WAITING ON THE LORD IN PRAYER

ZACHARIAS TANEE FOMUM

Copyright © 1996 by Zacharias Tanee Fomum

All rights reserved.

No part of this book may be reproduced in any form or by any electronic or mechanical means, including information storage and retrieval systems, without written permission from the author, except for the use of brief quotations in a book review.

CONTENTS

Preface	v
1. Prayer	1
2. Prayerlessness	14
3. Some Biblical Proclamations on Waiting on God	22
4. Wating on The Lord in Prayer: Prayer, a Monologue?	24
5. True Praying is a Dialogue	32
6. Waiting on God in Prayer so as To Know God's Will	50
7. Waiting on God Instead of Turning To Man	70
8. Waiting on The Lord in Prayer: The Example of Moses on The Mountain - 1	76
9. Waiting on The Lord in Prayer: The Example of Moses on The Mountain - 2	91
10. Waiting on The Lord in Prayer: The Example of Moses on The Mountain - 3	101
11. Waiting on The Lord in Prayer: The Example of Moses on The Mountain - 4	112
12. Waiting on The Lord in Prayer: The Example of The 120 Disciples	121
13. Waiting on The Lord in Prayer: The Example of Erlo Stegen	127
14. Waiting on The Lord in Prayer: The Example of Saul of Tarsus - 1	132
15. Waiting on The Lord in Prayer: The Example of Saul of Tarsus - 2	138
16. A Prayer Meeting With Waiting on The Lord in Prayer	142
17. Waiting on The Lord in Prayer: The Example of The Lord Jesus	146
18. In Conclusion	149

Very Important!!!	151
Thank You	155
About the Author	157
Also by Z.T. Fomum	163
Distributors of ZTF Books	171

PREFACE

This book, «*Waiting on The Lord in Prayer*», is the ninth in the series : "The Prayer Power." The books in this series that have already been written are:

1. The Way of Victorious Praying
2. The Ministry of Fasting
3. The Art of Intercession4 The Practice of Intercession
4. Praying With Power[1]
5. Moving God Through Prayer
6. Practical Spiritual Warfare Through Prayer
7. The Ministry of Praise And Thanksgiving
8. Waiting on the Lord in Prayer

For many believers, prayer is coming to the Lord and throwing as many requests to Him as possible in the shortest possible time, and then rushing away. The next time, the same process may be repeated with other requests added, while some of the previous ones may be forgotten. This is unfortunate.

PREFACE

God ordained prayer primarily so that His needs be met. In the prayer that the Lord Jesus taught his disciples, the priority of prayer was to be His Name, His Kingdom, and His Will.

> «Our Father in heaven, hallowed be <u>your name</u>, <u>your kingdom</u> come, <u>your will</u> be done on earth as it is in heaven. Give us today our daily bread. Forgive us our debts, as we also have forgiven our debtors. And lead us not into temptation, but deliver us from the evil one» (Matthew 6:9-13).

If the priority in prayer are His name; His kingdom and His will, then it is obvious that for anyone to pray to the satisfaction of God, that one must come before God and wait before God, so that God should give him revelations as to what the needs of His Name, His Kingdom and His Will are. Until these are revealed by God to man, man cannot pray rightly. After they are revealed to man, man can begin to pray what God would have him pray about. This makes waiting on the Lord in prayer a must; for without waiting on the Lord in prayer there is no other way by which these things can be known.

The other issue is that we do not know what our real needs are. We may think that we know what we need, but a closer look will betray our ignorance. Only God knows what our true needs are. Faced with the issues of choosing a wife or a career, we have to face the fact that although we may know what we need now, we do not know what we shall need five, ten, twenty or fifty years from today. God knows what we shall need all the years of our lives. If we wait on Him to reveal to us what we shall always need so that we can ask what will meet our short and long term needs, then we shall be the

PREFACE

happier for it. This again makes waiting on the Lord in prayer a must.

The third thing we want to say is that unless people spend time together, they will not know each other much. Those who want to know the Lord must wait on Him in prayer, so that He may reveal Himself ever increasingly to them. The more a person waits on the Lord, the more the Lord will reveal Himself to that one; and the more revelations the person has from the Lord of His character, His will, His plans, His purposes, etc., the more the person will know the Lord. This again makes waiting on the Lord in prayer a must; for without such waiting, the believer will only have a superficial knowledge of Him.

We send this book out with prayer that the many believers who are being awakened to a life of praying, and are actually praying, learn to wait on the Lord in prayer and so pray more correctly. We send this book out with prayer that since it is a matter of Waiting On The Lord In Prayer, the saints should not just wait in prayer, but they should wait on the Lord in prayer. That is, they should wait and wait and keep waiting until the Lord has spoken or answered.

We are well aware of the fact that as in all aspects of spiritual science there is an initiation, a learning and a continuation as progress is made, those who do not yet wait on the Lord in prayer will enrol in the School Of Waiting On The Lord In Prayer, and make progress.

We commend you, dear reader, as we commend this book, to the Lord of glory with prayer that He be glad to use this book for your spiritual enrichment.

To Him be all the honour and glory!

Amen.

PREFACE

Zacharias TANEE FOMUM,
P.O. Box 6090, Yaounde, Cameroon.
16th April, 1996

---

1. Formally published as ***With Christ in the School and Ministry of Praying.***

«It is very important to listen to God. A man came to see me. He talked for an hour about his troubles. The next week he came again and I talked to him for an hour. The next week he came to see me again. I said to him, 'The first time you talked for an hour. The second time I talked for an hour. Now, let us give everyone a chance to talk. Let us be silent and let God tell us what He wants to say.' After an hour of silence God was able to show this man how to solve his problems.»

— PAUL TOURNIER

«Let any man shut himself up for a week with only bread and water, with no book except the Bible, with no visitor except the Holy Spirit, and I guarantee (you) my preaching brethren, that that man will either break up or break through and out . After that, like Paul, he will be known in hell!»

— LEONARD RAVENHILL

PRAYER

"Ask and it will be given to you; seek and you will find; knock and the door will be opened to you. For everyone who asks receives; he who seeks finds; and to him who knocks, the door will be opened"(Matthew 7:7-8).

«Therefore I tell you, whatever you ask in prayer, believe that you have received it, and it will be yours. And when you stand praying, if you hold anything against anyone, forgive him, so that your Father in heaven may forgive your sins» (Mark 11:24-25).

«And will not God bring about justice for his chosen ones, who cry out to Him day and night? Will he keep putting them off? I tell you, he will see that they get justice, and quickly» (Luke 18:7-8).

«Be always on the watch, and pray that you may be able to escape all that is about to happen, and that you may be able to stand before the Son of man»(Luke 21:36).

«And I will do all that you ask in my name, so that the Son may bring glory to the Father. You may ask me for anything in my name, and I will do it" (John 14:13-14).

"So the twelve gathered all the disciples together and said, 'It would not be right for us to neglect the ministry of the word of God in order to wait on tables. Brothers, choose seven men among you who are known to be full of the Spirit and wisdom. We will turn this responsibility over to them and we will give our attention to prayer and the ministry of the word'" (Acts 6: 2-4).

Now that Pentecost had fallen, it might be thought that the Apostles could relax and dispense with so much emphasis on prayer. But not so. These specially chosen and anointed men realised that their warfare was not one of flesh and blood, but a continual warfare in the heavenlies. They had had an ample opportunity in Christ's school of prayer to know how He drew His power through day-to-day communion with God. Now, they -the Apostles- would institute a regular hour of prayer. In fact, Peter and John were on their way to the Temple to attend this hour of prayer when the first great miracle of the early church occurred - the healing of the lame man at the Gate Beautiful. "Now, Peter and John went up together to the temple at the hour of prayer, being the ninth hour" (Acts 3:1).

Here we pause a moment to emphasize something of supreme importance. People are creatures of habit. Hit and miss prayer, in the long run, never produces any satisfactory results. There must be a regular hour for it, otherwise the pressures of daily duties will press in, and before long we may find that the spirit of prayer has left us. Omit prayer for two or three days and at once we feel less inclined to pray. From the beginning, the Apostles appointed an hour for prayer. It was held at the ninth hour of the day - three o'clock in the afternoon. While morning is the best hour for an individual's devotions, for a group of people under various responsibilities, another time may be best. The important thing is that the hours be regular. That the thousands of new converts, who began to flow into the church, also participated in the prayer hour, is evident.

«Then, they that gladly received his word were baptized: and the same day there were added unto them about three thousand souls. And they continued steadfast in the Apostles' doctrine and fellowship, and in breaking of bread and in prayers» (Acts 2:41-42).

With this mighty united source of prayer ascending to heaven, the church moved forward, overcoming all opposition. Five thousand in one day accepted Christ as Lord ! (Acts4:3-4). For this, the Apostles were thrown in jail. On the morrow, they were threatened and let go. Upon returning to their own company, they reported what had happened. Immediately this great company gathered in its regular time of prayer *«and lifted up their voice to God in one accord» (Acts 4:24).*

— GORDON LINDSAY, «PRAYING TO CHANGE THE WORLD,» VOLUME 2, DALLAS, TEXAS, USA

«Jesus was not speaking in fables and fairy tales when he said to His disciples in Matthew 5:13-14: «Ye are the salt of the earth.» ; «Ye are the light of the world.» The world at large is totally blind to this fact, but if it were not for the purifying and preserving influence of the church, the fabric of all we call civilization would totally disintegrate, decay and disappear. At this present throbbing moment, the Church, in union with her risen and enthroned Lord is , therefore, the fundamental preserving factor in this present world order. Therefore, by virtue of her organic relationship with Christ, the Supreme Sovereign, she, not Satan holds the balance of power in

human affairs. It has been truly said, «The fate of the world is in the hands of nameless saints.» The truth is wonderfully set forth in Psalm 149:5-9: «Let the saints be joyful in glory; let them sing aloud upon their beds. Let the high praises of God be in their mouths, and a two-edged sword in their hands, to execute the vengeance upon the heathen, and punishment upon the people, to bind their kings with chains, and their nobles with fetters of iron; to execute upon them the judgment written. This honour have all the saints. Praise the Lord.» If it were not for the church, Satan would already have turned this earth into hell. The fact that it has been preserved from total devastation in spite of him, proves that at least a remnant of the Church is effectually functioning and already has entered upon her rulership in union with her Lord. She is even now, by virtue of the scheme of prayer and faith, engaged in 'on-the-job' training for her place as co-sovereign with Christ over the entire universe following Satan's final destruction... The validity of these principalities in world affairs at large is fairly well documented. But are these principles applicable in personal and individual cases? In the instance of the salvation of a specific individual, who holds the balance of power, Satan or the Church? Does the authority which God has offered the Church reach into the domain of free moral agency? Is this delegated authority compatible with the free will? God has said in His Word that He wills that all be saved. Knowing that it is God's Will to save any man who has not crossed that mysterious boundary known as the deadline, may the Church pray for the salvation of a specific individual in the assurance that he will be saved? Or must the Church's faith be tempered by the fact that that person is a free moral agent, and that God never saves any man against his will? Must we say, as we so often do, that because 'so and so' is a free moral agent, all we can do is to pray and leave the rest to him and God? Since God has assured us that it is His Will that all men be saved, we therefore know that when we pray for the salvation of anyone who has not crossed the deadline of final and permanent impertinence, we are praying according to His Will. In 1 John 5:4-5, the Apostle says, «And this is the confidence that we have in him, that, if we ask anything according to His Will, he heareth us, and if we know that he hear us, whatsoever we ask, we know that we have the petitions that we desired of him.» Now, the question is: Is this promise neutralised by the free moral agency of man? Do we have to stand back and watch Satan capture a soul because God does not save against His will? Is it correct to say that all we can do is to pray and leave the rest to God and the individual?

May I answer that question by asking another? Do you believe that someone was ever saved who was not, in the beginning, a rebel? Were not all of us born with our backs against God? Did we not all, like Adam, run and hide from God? Did we not all mightily resist the wooing of God's Spirit before we were saved? And did we not all continue to resist that wooing until it became so persuasive and compelling that it finally became easier to yield than to continue in that rebellion? Did there not come a point when rebellion crossed over into surrender, not because the will was coerced, but because it was more painful to resist than to yield? And although the will yielded, it could have, if it had chosen, continued in rebellion. Is not this the general pattern of the journey from rebellion to surrender? Jesus says,

«*No man can come to me except the Father ...draw him*» *(John 6:44).*

And the Father always draws by means of His Spirit. Since God is no respecter of persons and wills that all be saved, and therefore without exception seeks all (John 1:9), why is the Spirit's wooing successful in some cases and not in others? Is it because in some instances God is so 'powerless' that He cannot prevail? Or is it that some are the subjects of powerful, importunate, and believing intercession while others have no one to pray for them? If Wesley is correct in saying that «God does nothing but in answer to prayer,» then, this must include the salvation of souls. This then means that no soul is saved apart from intercession, and that every soul which is saved, is saved because someone prayed who would not give up to Satan. We agree that God desires all men to be saved. He has made provision for the salvation of all.

«Behold the Lamb of God, which taketh away the sin of the world» (John 1:29).

«And he is the propitiation for our sins, and not for ours only but also for the sins of the whole world» (1 John 2:2).

Although it is God's will that all be saved, and although He has made provision for the salvation of the whole world, this salvation is limited wholly and entirely by the intercession, or lack of it of the church. Those for whom the church travails are saved. All the others are lost.

«And when He had said this, He breathed on them, and said to them, Receive ye the Holy Ghost; whose soever sins ye remit, they are remitted unto them, and whose soever sins ye retain, they are retained»(John 20:22-23).

"The Holy Spirit has the power to so enlighten the mind, awaken the spirit, and move the emotions of a man that he will find it easier to yield than to continue in his rebellion. God will not go over the head of His Church even to have a soul without her co-operation. If she will not intercede, the Holy Spirit, by His own choice, cannot do His office work of convicting and persuading. By virtue of His purpose to qualify His Bride for her eternal rulership with Him, He has chosen to save no soul until she travails.

«The Spirit and the bride say, Come» Revelation 22:17).

Not the Spirit alone, but the Spirit and the Bride. He will do nothing without her. Hence he can do nothing without her.

If she does not travail, the Spirit does not woo. If the Spirit does not woo, the soul is lost. But the Spirit can and will woo; He can and will persuade any soul who has not crossed the deadline, for whom the church travails.

This being so, then, the church, not Satan, holds the balance of power not only in world affairs but in the salvation of individual souls. Therefore a holy Church, by her intercession or lack of it, holds the power of life or death over the souls of men. Without violating a person's free moral agency (full moral responsibility), the Spirit can so powerfully persuade that soul that he will voluntarily yield. But he does this only in answer to believing prayer and intercession of a believing church."

— PAUL E. BILLHEIMER, «DESTINED FOR THE THRONE» C.L.C. LONDON, GREAT BRITAIN

"Prayer is hardly ever mentioned in the Bible alone, it is prayer and earnestness; prayer and watchfulness, prayer and thanksgiving. It is an instructive fact that throughout scripture prayer is always linked with something else. Bartimeus was in earnest, and the Lord heard his cry."

— D.L. MOODY

"Nothing is more pleasing to our Father in heaven than direct, importunate, and persevering prayer. Two christian ladies, whose husbands were unconverted, feeling their great danger, agreed to

spend one hour each day in united prayer for their salvation. This was continued for seven years when they debated whether they should pray longer, so useless did their prayers appear. They decided to persevere till death, and if their husbands went to destruction, it should be laden with prayers. In renewed strength, they prayed three years longer, when one of them was awakened in the night by her husband, who was in great distress for sin. As soon as the day dawned, she hastened, with joy, to tell her praying companion that God was about to answer their prayers. What was her surprise to meet her friend coming to her house on the same errand! Thus, ten years of united and persevering prayer was crowned with the conversion of both husbands on the same day."

— D.L. MOODY

"*We cannot be too frequent in our requests; God will not weary of His children's' prayers. Sir Walter Raleigh asked a favour of Queen Elizabeth, to which she replied, 'Raleigh, when will you leave off begging?' 'When your majesty leaves off giving,' he replied. So long must we continue praying.»*

— D.L. MOODY

"*Sweet is the precious gift of prayer,*

To bow before the throne of grace

To leave our every burden there;

And gain new strength to run the race;

To gird our heavenly armour on,

Depending on the Lord alone."

— AUTHOR UNKNOWN

"I would a thousand times have rather that God's will should be done than my own. I cannot see into the future as God can; therefore it is a good deal better to let Him choose for me than to choose for myself. I know His mind about spiritual things. His will is that I should be sanctified; so I can with confidence pray to God for that, and expect an answer to my prayers. But when it comes to temporal matters, it is difficult; what I ask for may not be God's purpose concerning me.

As one has well put it: «Depend upon it, prayer does not mean that I am to bring God down to my thoughts and my purposes, and bend His government according to my foolish, silly, and sometimes sinful notions. Prayer means that I am to be raised up to feeling, into unity and design with Him, that I am to enter into His counsel, and carry out His purpose fully."

— D.L. MOODY IN "PREVAILING PRAYER"
MOODY PRESS, CHICAGO, USA

"The believing man resorts to God at all times, that he may keep up his relationship with the Divine mind. Prayer is not a soliloquy, but a dialogue, not an introspection, but a looking towards the hills, whence cometh our health."

— *C.H. SPURGEON*

"Let us remember that when we pray we ought to expect an answer. Let us be looking for it."

— *D.L. MOODY*

"Since I began to beg God's blessings on my studies, I have done more in one week than in the whole year before."

— PAYSON

"Satan trembles when he sees the weakest saint upon his knees."

"Prayer is a fiercely contested conflict. Satan is a trained strategist, and an obstinate fighter. He refuses to acknowledge defeat until he must. It is the fight for his life. The enemy yields only what he must. He yields only what is taken. Therefore, the ground must be taken step by step. He continually renews his attacks, therefore the ground taken must be held against him in the Victor's Name."

— S.D. GORDON

"Prayer is a contest of wills. If Satan's will, persistence, and determination outlast that of the petitioner, the petitioner is defeated. But the petitioner has the advantage because of Christ's victory and never needs to suffer defeat. Importunity combined with perfect faith is unconquerable."

— S.D. GORDON

"The work of God's people is to pray."

— ARTHUR MATTHEWS

"All prayer first begins with God before it is taken up on earth. His will is the only focus of all true prayer. He has been over all circumstances that make up the situation and knows what needs to be done. But he restrains action until a call reflecting His will comes from earth. Only the prayer that finds its expression through a will that is captive to His desiring can be assured of its hearing at the Throne of Grace. To achieve this, God sometimes arranges a set of

circumstances that will lay a burden of constraint on someone to direct specific prayer towards the particular thing He is wanting to accomplish. The Spirit-sensitized soul seeking after God's will in the circumstances becomes aware of what God is aiming to do, so gives himself to prayer to seek its accomplishment."

— *ARTHUR MATTHEWS, «BORN FOR BATTLE» SCRIPTURE UNION PRESS, IBADAN, NIGERIA.*

"God touched our weary bodies with His power,

And gave us strength for many a trying hour

In which we might have faltered

Had not you, our intercessors,

Faithful been and true.

Because you prayed,

God touched our eager fingers with His skill,

Enabling us to do His blessed will

With scalpel, sutune, bandage - better still

He healed the sick and wounded, cured the ill.

Because you prayed, God touched our lips with coals from altar fire,

Gave Spirit fullness, and did so inspire

That when we spoke , sin-blinded souls did see,

Sin's chains were broken - captives were set free.

Because you prayed,

The dwellers in the dark have found light;

The glad good news has banished heathen night;

The message of the cross so long delayedHas brought them life at last because you prayed."

— LEONARD RAVENHILL, «REVIVAL GOD'S WAY» BETHANY HOUSE PUBLISHERS, MINEAPOLIS, USA

«I was almost always in ejaculatory prayer wherever I was. Prayer seemed to be natural to me as the breath by which the inward burnings of the heart had vent.»

— *JONATHAN EDWARDS*

In 1607, William Gouge was ordained to the ministry. A year later, he became pastor of the church at Blackfriars, London, England. There he laboured for 45years. For 35 of those years he preached a midweek sermon on Hebrews. A biographer wrote: «Being very conscious of how he spent his time, he always would rise early, long before daylight, and would have completed his devotions by 4a.m.». And what a prayer warrior was Gouge -- «His confessions were accompanied with brokenness of heart, self-abhorrence. In petition, he accompanied faith with fervour. He, like a true son of Jacob, wrestled with tears and supplications, resolving not to let God go without a blessing.»

— *RAVENHILL*

"*Samuel Rutherford was one of the most learned men of his age. He commonly rose at three in the morning.*"

WAITING ON THE LORD IN PRAYER

— *RAVENHILL*

"No man can be a giant in prayer and a wealding in ministry."

— *RAVENHILL*

Pray or perish

— *THE AUTHOR*

2
PRAYERLESSNESS

«In the 39th year of his reign Asa was afflicted with a disease in his feet. Though this disease was severe, even in his illness he did not seek help from the Lord, but only from the physicians. Then in the 41st year of his reign Asa died and rested with his fathers»

— 2 CHRONICLES 16:12-13

"A church without an intelligent, well organised, and systematic prayer programme is simply operating a religious treadmill."

— BILLHEIMER

«The average local church provides an intelligent educational programme through the Sunday school and such auxiliaries as the Vacation Bible School. It may provide well-directed youth programmes, including social activities and recreational Bible camps. It may sponsor Teacher Training and Personal Evangelism classes. Many churches launch great evangelistic campaigns, featuring big-name evangelistic parties with a high potential of

religious entertainment. Many have an efficient, well-structured and highly successful stewardship and financial programme. All of those may be working smoothly and in high gear.

This is not to discount any of these programmes per se. They may be good. But if they are substitutes for any effective prayer programme, they may be useless so far as damaging Satan's kingdom is concerned."

— BILLHEIMER

"If we could see as God sees, we could behold a great forest of giant ecclesiastical treadmills operating in depth, all over the United States and in many other parts of the world. Such an operation may be very exhilarating. It may employ enormous man-power, absorb almost limitless time, and demand a huge financial budget. It may give an illusion of accomplishment and success. It may flatter the ego. But any church programme, no matter how impressive, if it is not supported by an adequate prayer programme, is little more than an ecclesiastical treadmill. It is doing little or no damage to Satan's kingdom."

— *PAUL E. BILLHEIMER «DESTINED FOR THE THRONE» C.L.C. LONDON, GREAT BRITAIN.*

"An arrow, if it be drawn up but a little way, goes not far; but, if it be pulled up to the head, flies swiftly and pierces deep. Thus prayer, if it be only dribbled forth from careless lips, falls at our feet. It is in the strength of ejaculation and a strong desire which sends it to heaven, and makes it pierce like the clouds. It is not the arithmetic of our prayers, how many they are; nor the rhetoric of our prayers, how eloquent they may be; nor the geometry of our prayers, how long they

may be; nor the music of our prayers, how sweet our voice may be; nor the logic of our prayers, how argumentative they may be; nor the method of our prayers, how orderly they may be; nor the divinity of our prayers, how good the doctrine may be ; which God cares for. He looks not for the horny knees which James is said to have had through the assiduity of prayer. We might be like Bartholomew, who is said to have had a hundred prayers for the morning, and as many for the evening, and all might be of no avail. Fervency of spirit is that which avails much."

— *HALL*

"It is not the gilded paper and good writing of a petition that prevails with a king, but the moving sense of it. And to that King who discerns the heart, heart-sense is the sense of all, and that which He only regards. He listens to hear what that speaks, and takes all as nothing where that is absent. All other excellence in prayer is but the outside and fashion of it. This is the life of it.»

— *LEIGHTON*

"As a painted fire is no fire, a dead man no man, so a cold prayer is no prayer. In a painted fire there is no heat, in a dead man there is no life; so in a cold prayer there is no omnipotence, no devotion, no blessing. Cold prayers are as arrows without heads, as swords without edges, as birds without wings; they pierce not, they cut not, they fly not up to heaven. Cold prayers do always freeze before they get up to heaven. Oh that Christians would chide themselves out of their cold prayers, and chide themselves into a better and warmer frame of spirit, when they make their supplications to the Lord!»

— *BROOKS*

«Easiness of desire is a great enemy to the success of a good man's prayer. It must be an intense, zealous, busy operative prayer; for consider what a huge indecency it is that a man should speak to God for a thing that he values not!. Our prayers upbraid our spirits when we beg lamely for those things for which we ought to die, which are more precious than imperial sceptres, richer than the spoils of the sea, or the treasures of Indian hills.»

— TAYLOR

"If I omit praying and reading God's Word in the morning, nothing goes well all day."

— *SIR MATTHEW HALE*

"Satan can get along very well with believers as long as they are on the defensive, seeking détente or deserting. Therefore, if we are determined to see him defeated in our hearts and in our society, we must be only and always committed to the offensive."

— *ARTHUR MATTHEWS*

"One reason why many prayers are apparently unanswered is the failure of the petitioner to continue with importunity until the answer is recovered."

— *BILLHEIMER*

Today, deacons and elders are usually «men of standing». In the New Testament church, they were «men of kneeling» praying men. Who checks the prayer life of the men to be elected? Usually no one. In other words, we will choose whom we want and hope that the Lord will mercifully bless us."

— *RAVENHILL*

"Our spiritual immaturity never shows up more than in our lack of praying, be it alone or in a church prayer meeting. Let 20% of the choir members fail to turn up for the rehearsals and the choir master is offended. Let 20% of the church members turn up for a prayer meeting, and the pastor is elated."

— *RAVENHILL*

"On the highways I see buses with signs on the sides such as «AAA Church Choir on Tour,» or «BBB Bible College Choir on Tour,» but I never see a bus announcing «CCC Church Prayer Meeting on Tour».

— *RAVENHILL*

"There are churches with a Senior Minister, Associate Minister, Minister of Music, Minister of Youth, and Minister of Education, but where is there a church with a Minister of prayer, where is there a church with a room marked: «Quiet. Intercessors at Work»? (For prayer is work!)"

— *RAVENHILL*

"Prayer in its highest form is agonising soul sweat. Prayer is not just casting off a burden. It is having sense enough, and heart enough to ask God to share the burdens of His great heart with me."

— *RAVENHILL*

"Man is born to choices, decisions, and options. I can choose this day to pray or not to pray, to fast or not to fast. Yesterday's choices are gone. Tomorrow's choices are unborn. This is the day!!"

— *RAVENHILL*

"Without prayer, man is not truly man."

— *CHARLES WHINSTON*

"In what ways is our praying different from that of a Jew, a Moslem, or a Hindu?. Should there not be unique marks to christian praying? Do our prayers use God or offer ourselves to God that He may use us? How many of our prayers are egocentric, seeking our own gain, and how few are devoted to serving God! Are we willing to face the penetrating judgment of Jesus Christ upon our basically pagan praying?"

— *CHARLES WHINSTON*

"One of the major reasons why we give up praying is that we lack any secure foundation for our praying. Prayer that is enduring and stable must be built upon rocklike foundations."

— *CHARLES WHINSTON*

"The life of christian praying will never be easy. Nothing that is truly important is easy. But that does not mean that it is not possible for every person to have an authentic life of prayer."

— *CHARLES WHINSTON*

"More study about prayer is not sufficient. It is the practice of prayer that brings ideas to life."

— *[CHARLES WHINSTON: "PRAY: A STUDY OF DISTINCTIVE CHRISTIAN PRAYING" WILLIAM B. EERDMANS PUBLISHING*

COMPANY, GRAND RAPIDS, MICHIGAN, USA].

Even in specially called prayer meetings, where it would be supposed, the most spiritual persons in the community are present, many of the prayers are little more than pious monologues on current events. They are suggested by the news headlines rather than inspired by the Spirit. They cover the earth like clouds without rain, promising much and delivering little.

To pray effectively we must want what God wants - that and only that is to pray in the will of God. And no petition made in the will of God was ever refused."

— A.W. TOZER, «LEANING INTO THE WIND» KINGSWAY PUBLICATION LTD, SUSSEX, GREAT BRITAIN

"I often think of this when I observe the situation in the christian enterprise of today. That the machinery has become too heavy is because we are operating it with human labour instead of running it by power from above. I know fully well that there is not a little individual, as well as united prayer. But I am afraid that we do not put real work into prayer and that we do not, therefore, put our trust in the power of God when it is a question of carrying on and carrying forward our work. And for that reason our christian work becomes so strenuous and so exhausting.

The powers of heaven are at our disposal. Have we made the proper contacts with these powers? Let us pray for the Spirit of prayer. He will take us into the workshop where the power conduits lie. Above the door of this room is written: 'Nothing shall be impossible unto you.' The future of the christian work which is now being carried on with such great intensity does not depend on curtailment or reorganisation. It depends on whether the Spirit of God can persuade us to take up the work of prayer."

> — [O. HALLESBY, «PRAYER,» INTER-VARSITY FELLOWSHIP, LONDON, GREAT BRITAIN.]

SOME BIBLICAL PROCLAMATIONS ON WAITING ON GOD

1. *"Yea, let none that wait on thee be ashamed: let them be ashamed which transgress without cause"* (Psalm 25: 3 KJV).
2. *"Lead me in thy truth, and teach me: for thou art the God of my salvation; on thee do I wait all the day"* (Psalm 25:5 KJV).
3. *"Wait on the Lord, be of good courage, and he shall strengthen thine heart: Wait, I say, on the Lord"* (Psalm 27:14 KJV).
4. *"Be still before the Lord and wait patiently for him; do not fret when men succeed in their ways, when they carry out their wicked schemes"* (Psalm 37:7).
5. *"My soul, wait thou only upon God: for my expectation is from him"* (Psalm 62: 5 KJV).
6. *"I am weary of my crying: my throat is dried, mine eyes fail while I wait for my God"* (Psalm 69: 3 KJV).
7. *"Let not them that wait on thee, O Lord God of hosts, be ashamed for my sake: Let not them that seek thee be confounded for my sake, O God of Israel"* (Psalm 69: 6, KJV).

8. *"I wait for the Lord, my soul waits, and in his word I put my hope. My soul waits for the Lord more than watchmen wait for the morning, more than watchmen wait for the morning" (Psalm 130: 5-6).*
9. *"I will wait for the Lord, who is hiding his face from the house of Jacob. I will put my trust in him" (Isaiah 8:17).*
10. *"Yet the Lord longs to be gracious to you; He rises to show you compassion. For the Lord is a God of justice. Blessed are all who wait for him!" (Isaiah 30:18)*
11. *"The Lord is good unto them that wait for him, to the soul that seeketh him. It is good that a man should both hope and quietly wait for the salvation of the Lord" (Lamentation 3:25-26 KJV)*
12. *"But you must return to your God; maintain love and justice, and wait for your God always" (Hosea 12:6).*
13. *"But as for me, I watch in hope for the Lord, I wait for God my Saviour; my God will hear me" (Micah 7:7).*

4

WATING ON THE LORD IN PRAYER: PRAYER, A MONOLOGUE ?

For many believers, prayer is a monologue. They come running into God's presence and throw some words at Him, which may include the following:

1. *Lord, I praise You.*
2. *Lord, I bless You.*
3. *Lord, I worship You.*
4. *Lord, I magnify Your name.*
5. *Lord, I need You.*
6. *Lord, give me power to serve You.*
7. *Lord, forgive my many sins against You.*
8. *Lord, heal me of the pain in my back.*
9. *Lord, bless our evangelistic meeting of today.*
10. *Lord, grant that many people come and that many be saved.*
11. *Lord, give me money for a new dress.*
12. *Lord, give me money for the payment of my rents in three days' time.*
13. *Lord, bless our son in school. Cause him to be among the first three.*
14. *Lord, help me to walk close to You.*

15. *Amen.*

They have carried out a monologue. They have said what they wanted to say to God and after that they have gone away.

PRAYER AS A MONOLOGUE: MAN ALONE SPEAKS

In prayer as a monologue, man alone speaks. The first thing that is wrong with this kind of praying is that man may be praying to himself. The person who is praying has not laboured to create contact with God. He has not laboured to pluck into God. There may be sin in his life which has not been confessed, forsaken and forgiveness sought and received from the Lord. If there is such a sin or if there are such sins, the praying is a waste of time, because God will not listen to it. About this matter the Lord said,

> "When you spread out your hands in prayer, I will hide my eyes from you; even if you offer many prayers, I will not listen. Your hands are full of blood; wash and make yourselves clean. Take your evil deeds out of my sight! Stop doing wrong" (Isaiah 1:15-16).

The Psalmist proclaimed,

> "If I had cherished sin in my heart, the Lord would not have listened; but God has surely listened and heard my voice in prayer. Praise be to God, who has not rejected my prayer or withheld his love from me!" (Psalm 66:18-20).

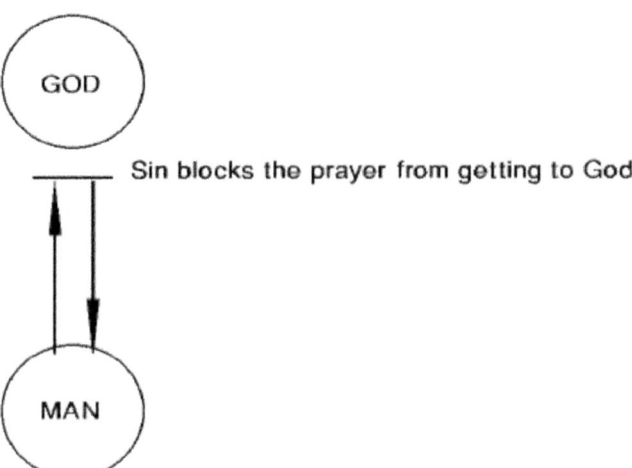

PRAYER AS A MONOLOGUE. MAN PRAYS BUT GOD DOES NOT HEAR HIM.

A man can be blocked by sin for many days, months, years, and yet continue to pray prayers that do not get to God. The prayers leave his lips, bounce on his sin and come back to him. Because he is separated from God by his sin, he may not realise that his prayers are getting nowhere and so he continues with his monologues and may even increase the quantity and intensity of them. All is in vain. The Bible says,

> "In the fourth year of king Darius, the word of the Lord came to Zechariah on the fourth day of the ninth month, the month of Kislev. The people of Bethel had sent Sharezer and Regem-Melech, together with their men, to entreat the Lord by asking the priests of the house of the Lord Almighty and the prophets, "<u>Should I mourn and fast in the fifth month, as I have done for so many years?</u> " <u>The word of the Lord Almighty came to me:</u> "<u>Ask all the people of the land and the priests, 'When you fasted and mourned in the fifth and seventh months for the past seventy years, was it really for me that you fasted?</u> And when you were eating and drinking, were you not just feasting for yourselves?'....And the word of the Lord came again to Zechariah:
>
> "This is what the Lord Almighty says: 'Administer true justice; show mercy and compassion to one another. Do not oppress the widow or the fatherless, the alien or the poor. <u>In your hearts do not think evil of each other</u>'" (Zechariah 7:1-10).

For seventy years, these people fasted two whole months each year. They invested 140 fasting months, yet it was not received by the Lord. The Lord said that it was not really for Him that they fasted. Outwardly, it looked as if they were fasting for the Lord. However, the reality was that they were fasting for themselves. There was sin in their lives and this made the fasts unacceptable to God.

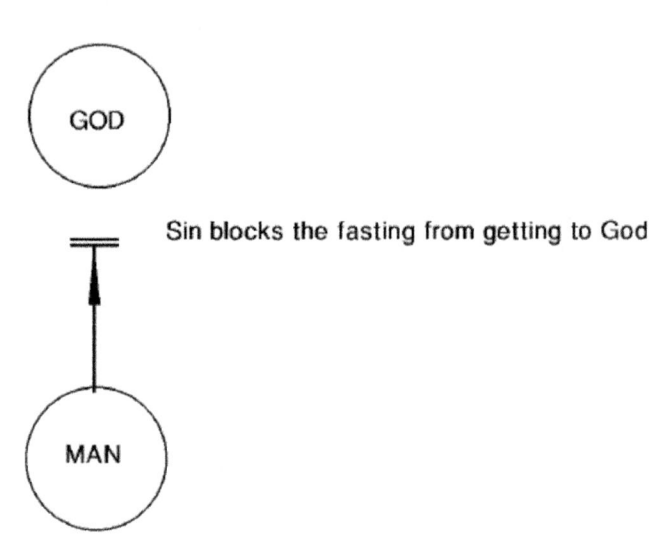

FASTING AS A MONOLOGUE. MAN FASTS BUT GOD DOES NOT HEAR HIM.

These people fasted two months every year for seventy years. They thought they were doing very well. Year by year they went on with their monologue. They did not bother to check with God. They did not bother to bring God in. They were caught up with their activity and, instead of rejoicing in the Lord, they rejoiced in what they were doing "for Him."

There were a number of sins that separated them from the Lord and made their fasts unacceptable to God:

1. *Injustice.*
2. *Mercilessness.*
3. *Compassionlessness.*

4. *Oppression of the widow.*
5. *Oppression of the fatherless.*
6. *Oppression of the alien.*
7. *Oppression of the poor.*
8. *Evil thoughts about each other.*

All these eight things are serious things before God. Every sin is a serious thing before God. Even if the only sin that they had committed was that of having evil thoughts about each other, their fasts would have been unaccepted by God who looks at the heart.

There is much praying in some circles in our day and much fasting too. However, the results that are being produced by these prayers and fasting endeavours seem lamentably poor. The main reason for such insignificant answers to so much praying and fasting is that the prayers and fasts are not reaching God. They are bouncing on the sins in the hearts of the saints and making no progress God-ward.

If a man is blocked by sin and he prays for one hour, ten hours, one hundred hours, one thousand hours, or one million hours, he will get nowhere with God. When there is a block to prayer, many hours of praying will not remove the block.

The need of so many believers today is not to increase the quantity of their prayers, but to get right with God by confessing and forsaking the sin that separates them from God. When the barrier is removed, the quantity of prayer will then count.

Sin in the heart must be confessed, forsaken and forgiveness sought and received. The restored person can then pray and God will answer.

Another thing that is wrong with prayer as a monologue is that the person who carries out monologues may be blocked by sin and this will mean that even when others pray for him, the answers from the Lord cannot get to him because of his sin.

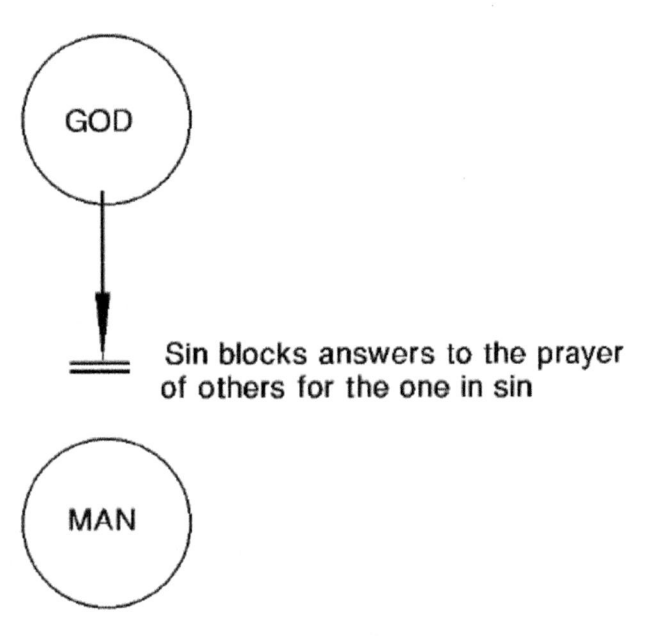

PRAYER AS A MONOLOGUE. THE ANSWERS OF THE PRAYERS ARE BLOCKED BY SIN

For the person for whom prayer is a monologue, he may go on praying and even asking others to pray for him without confronting the fact that it is not only his prayers that are blocked, but the prayers of others on his behalf are also blocked. If he waited on God, he might see what is wrong and remove the barrier. If, however, he would not wait, he will continue with a prayer life that may be active but is obviously barren.

1. *It is important that a person walk right in order to be able to pray rightly.*
2. *It is important that a person have a pure heart in order to pray and be heard.*
3. *All who harbour one sin or another in their hearts and pray are wasting their time.*
4. *Stop wasting your time.*
5. *Wait before the Lord in prayer.*
6. *Listen to Him.*
7. *Hear Him.*
8. *Obey Him.*
9. *Then pray to Him.*

The Psalmist proclaimed,

> "Hear, O Lord, my righteous plea; listen to my cry. <u>Give ear to my prayer - it does not rise from deceitful lips.</u> May my vindication come from you; may your eye see what is right. Though you probe my heart and examine me at night, though you test me, you will find nothing; <u>I have resolved that my mouth will not sin.</u> As for the deeds of men - by the word of your lips I have kept myself from the ways of the violent. My steps have held to your paths; my feet have not slipped. <u>I call on you, O God, for you will answer me, give ear to me and hear my prayer</u>" (Psalm 17: 1-6).

5

TRUE PRAYING IS A DIALOGUE

True praying is a dialogue.

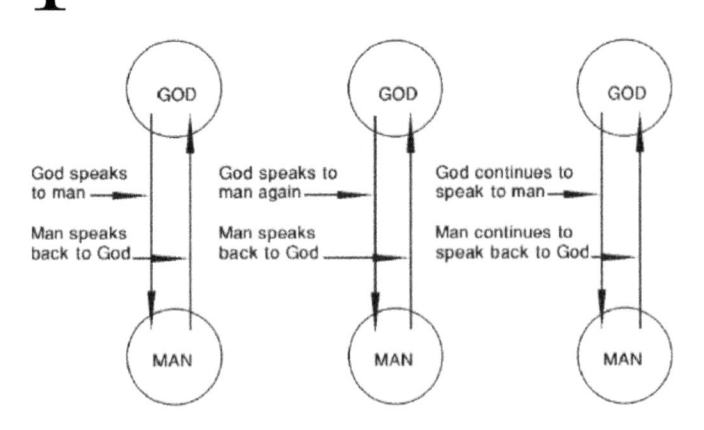

```
    GOD              GOD              GOD

God speaks      God speaks to    God continues to
to man →        man again →      speak to man →

Man speaks      Man speaks       Man continues to
back to God ←   back to God ←    speak back to God ←

    MAN              MAN              MAN
```

The dialogue could be initiated by God or by man. Normally speaking, when God initiates the dialogue, more profound things are shared than when man initiates the dialogue. When God initiates the dialogue, it is often to talk with man about the hallowing of His Name; His kingdom coming and His will being done on earth as it is in heaven. When man initiates the dialogue, it is often a matter of presenting some need associated with man's glory, man's kingdom and man's will being done.

As people advance in the things of God, they increasingly allow God to initiate the dialogue. They wait before God in prayer for Him to take the initiative. The immature can hardly wait. They have so many things of their own that they want to throw at God and rush away to something else. Waiting before God is an art of the mature. Dialogue in prayer is for those who are determined to have God's best and who have rejected His second best totally.

In this dialogue, the person who wants to pray comes into God's presence. When he comes into God's presence, the first thing that he does is to examine himself to see if he is in a condition in which God can talk to him or listen to him. We recommend the following formula for a quick check-up:

1. FORTUNE

Is there anything wrong in my relationship with money and all forms of worldly wealth? Is there any covetousness in my heart for anything? Am I desiring something that the Lord Jesus would not have desired, were He in my position today? Am I holding back some money which I ought to invest into the cause of the Gospel now? Am I keeping something which I do not really need, even though I know someone who needs it? Do I give a tithe and an offering regularly to God's work? Has the percentage of my offering been increasing as God has prospered me? What sum of money or property have I sacrificially given to the Lord? Is my life-style -- housing dressing and feeding -- simple? Are there any marks in my life-style that show that I care for those who have not heard the Gospel and I am prepared to inconvenience myself and invest more into the Gospel, so that they should be reached and saved?

As you go through these questions, you may find that you need to repent, confess your sin of the love of fortune to the Lord, forsake the sin and carry out restitution. This may take you hours or days. Do not hurry over things, because God does not want superficial dealings. Do not say that you will push some issues aside and pray first, and then see how you can handle them. It will not work. Your prayer will bounce on the wrong things in your relationship to fortune and come back to you. You will then have wasted time; for God will not have heard you. Consequently, it is best to get to grips with the issues that separate you from God, and get rid of them before you pray.

2. FEMALES/MALES

Is there anything wrong before God in your relationship with the opposite sex? Are your thoughts about every member of the opposite sex pure? Are your desires about every member of the opposite sex pure? Are you married but secretly desiring another member of the opposite sex to be your partner? Are your words, touches, looks and acts towards the opposite sex God-approved? The Lord Jesus said,

> "Any man who looks at a woman lustfully has already committed adultery with her in his heart"
> (Matthew 5:28).

Have you looked at someone lustfully? Who was the person? Did you confess that adulterous look to the Lord? Did you withdraw and confess to the Lord, "Lord, I have committed adultery in my heart with this person. I have defiled my heart which is Your dwelling place. I repent. I confess this sin to You and turn away from it and I will do everything in my power not to go back to it"? If you so confess, the Lord will forgive you and restore you and you can enter into His presence. Remember that if you committed such a sin in your heart and just brushed it aside, there is a barrier between you and God. Your prayers will bounce on that adultery committed in your heart and go nowhere. You will not only have to confess and forsake your sin of adultery in the heart. You will have to do everything to ensure that it does not happen again. The Lord Jesus counselled, "If your right eye causes you to sin, gouge it out and throw it away. It is better for you to lose one part of your body than for your whole body to be thrown into hell. And if your right hand causes you to sin, cut it off and throw it away. It is better for you to lose one part of your body than for your whole body to go into hell"(Matthew 5: 29-30) .

Job said,

> "I made a covenant with my eyes not to look lustfully at a girl"(Job 31:1).

You too should covenant with your eyes not to look at anyone of the opposite sex lustfully.

Are you living in a forbidden sexual relationship? Are you married to a divorced person? The Lord Jesus taught, saying,

> "The law and the prophets were proclaimed until John. Since that time, the good news of the kingdom of God is being preached, and everyone is forcing his way into it. It is easier for heaven and earth to disappear than for the least stroke of a pen to drop out of the law. Anyone who divorces

his wife and marries another commits adultery, and the man who marries a divorced woman commits adultery" (Luke 16:16-18).

Your adultery may be legalised by your nation or your denomination, but you are in trouble. God is not mocked. You cannot live in adultery and live in communion with God.

You may be living in masturbation. That too is against God. You cannot pray and be heard while you continue in that sin.

It may be good for you to take time and examine your life. Write down every immorality in motive, desire, thought, look, touch, word and act that you have ever committed and confess each to the Lord. If you do that, you will enter into a life of freedom, and the power of sexual immorality in your life will be broken deeply and permanently. You will then be able to enter into God's presence unhindered.

3. FAME

Why are you serving the Lord? Why are you doing the things that you are doing? Why are you dressing as you are dressing? Why are you buying the things you are buying? Why are you studying what you are studying? There are four possible reasons why you are doing what you are doing. You may be doing them solely for your own glory. You may be doing them mainly for your own glory and also for God's glory. You may be doing them mainly for God's glory, but partly for your own glory. You may be doing them solely for God's glory.

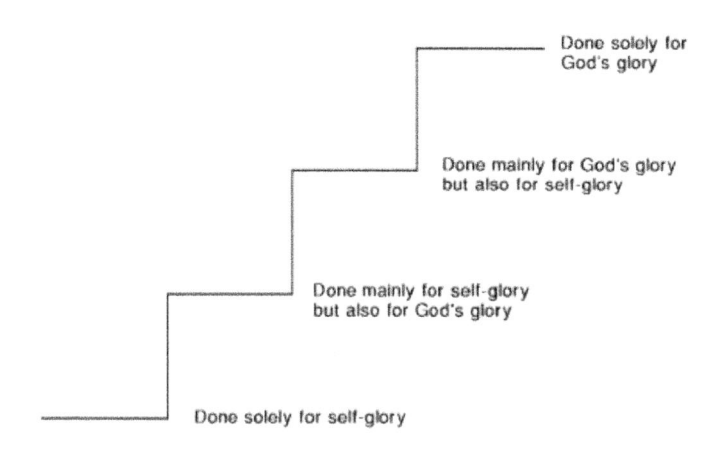

```
                              ─── Done solely for
                                   God's glory

                   ─── Done mainly for God's glory
                        but also for self-glory

         ─── Done mainly for self-glory
              but also for God's glory

─── Done solely for self-glory
```

If you are working for self-glory or partly for self-glory, you are blocked. The Holy Spirit is committed to the exaltation of Christ and the exaltation of Christ alone. All that has as its goal the exaltation of some person, some organisation, some denomination, etc. will fail to have His approval. The Lord Jesus said,

> "I do not accept praise from men" (John 5:41).

Those who seek the praise of men are working for self-glory. They can expect nothing from God. The Lord Jesus again asked,

> "How can you believe when you accept praise from one another, yet make no effort to obtain the praise that comes from the only God?» (John 5:44).

Anything that is done to be seen, praised and honoured by man is already rewarded by the praise obtained from man. No further praise can be expected at the Judgment Seat of Christ. All that is done to receive praise, congratulations and promotions from man immediately becomes wood, hay and stubble for that day!

Is there a secret desire to be

1. *seen,*
2. *noticed,*
3. *praised,*
4. *congratulated?*

Does your speech contain statements of

1. *self-praise,*
2. *self-exaltation,*
3. *self-promotion?*

Does your speech contain statements that

1. *belittle,*
2. *debase,*
3. *demote*

others? These are all marks of the love of fame. That love stands between the Lord and you, and you cannot get through to Him. It may look like a small matter to you, but the impact is serious.

```
     GOD
      |
   ___|___ Love of fame
      ^
      |
      |
     MAN
```

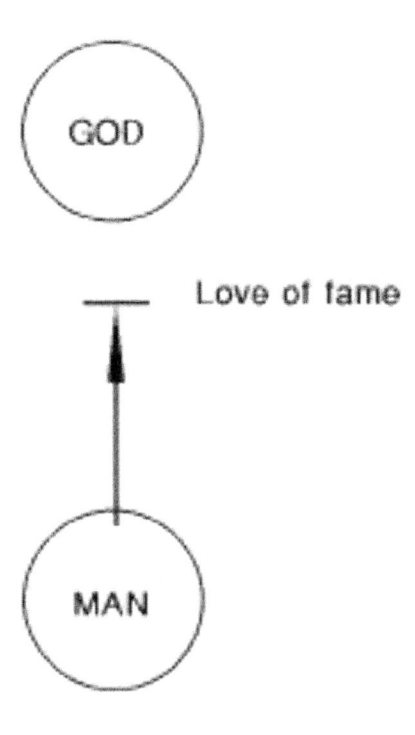

The Bible says, "To some who were confident of their own righteousness and looked down on everybody else, Jesus told this parable: "Two men went up to the temple to pray, one a Pharisee and the other a tax collector. The Pharisee stood up and prayed to himself: 'God, I thank you that I am not like other men - robbers, evil-doers, adulterers - or even like this tax collector. I fast twice a week and give a tenth of all I get.' But the tax collector stood at a distance. He would not even look up to heaven, but beat his breast and said, 'God, have mercy on me, a sinner."

"I tell you that this man, rather than the other, went home justified before God. For everyone who

exalts himself will be humbled, and he who
humbles himself will be exalted" (Luke 18 : 9-14.)

We repeat that all that is done for self-glory will appear that Day as wood, hay, and stubble, and there will be no reward for it. The Apostle Paul taught,

> "By the grace God has given me, I laid a foundation as an expert builder, and someone else is building on it. But each one should be careful how he builds. For no one can lay any foundation other than the one already laid, which is Jesus Christ. If any man builds on this foundation using gold, silver, costly stones, wood, hay or straw, his work will be shown for what it is, because the Day will bring it to light. It will be revealed with fire, and that fire will test the quality of each man's work. If what he has built survives, he will receive his reward. If it is burned up, he will suffer loss ; he himself will be saved, but only as one escaping through the flames" (1Corinthians 3: 10-15).

We repeat that all that is done for self-glory, however costly it may be, will be consumed on that Day as wood, hay and stubble. The person who serves or labours to receive the praise of men has already had his reward as men praise him.

The Lord Jesus taught, saying,

> "Be careful not to do your 'acts of righteousness' before men, to be seen by them. If you do, you will have no reward from your Father in heaven. So when you give to the needy, do not announce it with trumpets, as the hypocrites do in the

synagogues and in the streets, to be honoured by men. I tell you the truth, they have received their reward in full. But when you give to the needy, do not let your left hand know what your right hand is doing, so that your giving may be in secret. Then your Father, who sees what is done in secret, will reward you" (Matthew 6:1-4).

The statement: "They have received their reward in full," tells us in very clear terms that no reward will be received from the Lord on that Day or in the present.

This is a most serious thought, and it may be one of the principal reasons why prayers are unanswered. Self-love -- self-advertisement; self-promotion; self-preservation; self-praise; self-preservation, etc. -- stands in the way!

Are you prepared to confront this issue squarely? It may make the difference in time and eternity.

If you do not handle this issue radically and squarely, you have opted out of waiting on God in prayer, you have opted out of the real life of prayer, and you have opted out of God's blessings!

4 FALSEHOOD

Whenever falsehood is practised, a barrier is erected between man and God.

The falsehood could be in your relationship with your

1. *partner,*
2. *friend,*
3. *lover,*
4. *co-worker,*

5. *employer,*
6. *employee,*
7. *driver,*
8. *cook,*
9. *boss,*
10. *child,*
11. *parent,*
12. *student or teacher.*

The falsehood could be in your relationship with the handling of your personal finances, the handling of the finances of the church, the handling of the finances of the ministry, etc. The falsehood could be in your use of time, use of people, attitude to studies, etc. Whenever there is falsehood of any kind, unless it is recognised as sin that stands between man and God, confessed and forsaken at once and for all time, communion with God will be hindered and all efforts to pray wasted.

Are you prepared to be shown the falsehood of your heart? Are you prepared to face the falsehood of your will, mind and emotions? Are you prepared to be shown the falsehood of your prayers, fasts, Bible reading, meditations, giving to God, preaching, singing, exhortation? Are you willing to be shown the extent to which you have lied to yourself until you believe the lie? If you are prepared, take time away with God and give Him the opportunity to expose you as you are to yourself; so that you may know the extent to which you have been deceived or the extent to which you have deceived yourself.

There are four levels at which you can be seen:

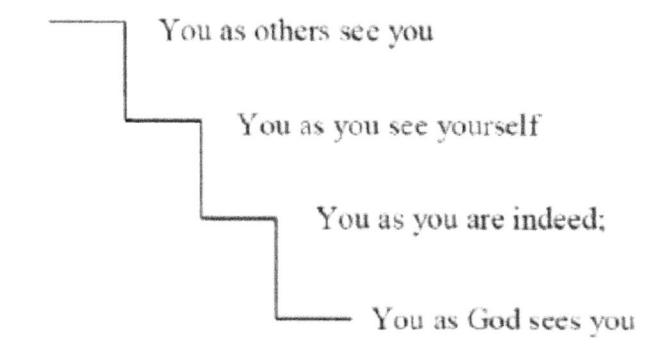

```
┌──── You as others see you
└──┐
   └── You as you see yourself
      └──┐
         └── You as you are indeed;
            └──┐
               └──── You as God sees you
```

The heart that wants the truth will want to see itself as God sees him and will want others to see him as God sees him. This is truth. Are you prepared to say to the Lord, "Expose me to myself as You see me and, Lord, help me to expose myself to others as I am indeed, i.e. as You see me"? That will be enrolment in the School Of Truth.

YOUR FIRST MAJOR EXPERIENCE OF WAITING ON GOD

If you are taking God seriously, you will not want to deceive yourself that you are praying to God when in reality your prayers are bouncing on some sin in your life. If you are taking God seriously, you will want to be sure that what is coming to you as God's voice is indeed God's voice, and not the deceitfulness of your heart.

To be sure, I encourage you to withdraw on a week-end from Friday evening to Sunday evening. You might have had a busy week or a busy day. I advise you to sleep first. Sleep for as long as you want. Then wake up and tell the Lord that you want to know yourself as He knows you in the critical domain of your relationship with money and worldly goods, in the realm of your relationship with the opposite sex, in the realm of fame and in the realm of falsehood. Plead with Him that although there are many things that separate you from Him, He should in His sovereignty create a way to talk to you so that you should change. Take a notebook and in great detail ask the Lord what He thinks about your bank account, your investments on earth, your investments in heaven, your lifestyle, the message that your possessions are proclaiming, the things you covet, the things you desire, the things you have but are unsatisfied, money earned fraudulently, those you have exploited, where you never carried out restitution when you believed, etc., etc. The Lord will show you things. Write them down. Write each one of them down. You may become tired and sleepy. Eat and sleep and wake up and plead with God to keep speaking to you. Plead with Him not to spare you any aspect of the truth. If you are forty years old, you may ask Him to show you what was wrong at the age of four, then at the age of five, then at the age of six, and so on until you come to the age of forty. You may want Him to show you where things were wrong in your attitude to your parents' finances and property; the property and funds of any club that you were a member of , the funds of the church or ministry, etc. If you find that the matter of having your heart exposed with respect to fortune is taking the entire weekend, be at peace. Plead with God that He should go on. Plead with Him that He should be particularly slow when He comes to the darkest areas of your life because, naturally, you would want to pass on quickly. Beg Him to help you to face the true ugliness of your heart and life. At some point it may be necessary to ask, "My Lord, is there not more to show me? I plead with You not to hold back anything. I prefer to face the truth now when I can still do something about it, than to wait until that day when the secrets of men's hearts shall be revealed and when it will be too late to do something about it."

When you ask the Lord to show you some more, linger in His presence. Wait for Him. Continue to beg Him to do the favour of showing you all.

Finally, the Lord will stop showing you things that are wrong in your attitude to fortune. You may also feel in your heart that He has shown you all that you can receive at that time. Thank Him for what He has shown you. Then read all that you wrote down as He was speaking, aloud in His presence and hearing. Then go away and plead with God that He should, in His mercy, cause you to hate all that is wrong. Go slowly from one thing to the other. Cry out to Him. Unless He gives you power to hate what is wrong, you cannot be delivered from it. People cannot be delivered from what they love. For deliverance, what they love must, first of all, be converted into what they hate, and then deliverance can take place.

Plead that God should give you the gift of godly sorrow, godly confession, godly forsaking of the sin, godly restitution, godly forgiveness and godly restoration.

If you find that the week-end is not enough to finish with fortune, set the next week-end apart for it. Give up all your other activities because they have essentially produced wood, hay and stubble for you. Do not fear being misunderstood. You want to get right with God. Does it matter what anyone else thinks about you or about how you are going about it? If you can continue on Monday, Tuesday, Wednesday and Thursday, please go on. The sooner you can get it done, the better for you. It may take two week-ends to handle fortune. It may also take two week-ends to handle each of the other three items - the opposite sex, fame and falsehood. When at last all is finished before God, you have a book of books of what you must put right with man. You will move from God's presence to executing what He has shown you. Again, ask Him to help you so that you do not jump over any practical issues. Plead with Him to help you not to accept the deception of your heart that says that God understands or that God does not expect you to be so detailed in your confession and restitution to man.

Maybe what happened to the man of God, John Tauler will happen to you.

> The story of John Tauler who in the fourteenth century was recognised as the greatest preacher of the age, is full of instruction. It was in 1331 that Tauler passed through the great crisis of his life. Had he not known what it was to be utterly rejected, and had he not been willing to drink the cup of humiliation and shame to its bitter dregs, he would never have known what it was to be fully accepted. The journal of those days is available, having been preserved by one of the select band known as 'The friends of God.' Tauler had announced that he would preach on the highest degree of perfection attainable in this life. The chapel of the famous Strasburg Cathedral was crowded long before the time of service, for multitudes hung upon the lips of Dr John Tauler. He preached on the necessity of dying utterly to the world, and to our own will, and of being yielded; what he described as 'dying - wise' into the hands of God.
>
> While he discoursed eloquently along these lines, there was one man in the congregation who knew that the preacher had but an imperfect personal knowledge of the truths on which he dwelt and that John Tauler was far from dead. This man was Nicholas of Basle, an eminent 'friend of God,' well-known in the Bernese Oberland as a saint of God possessed of profound spiritual insight and knowledge.

As he listened he said, "The master is a very loving, gentle, good-hearted man, but despite his understanding of Scripture, he is ignorant of the deep things of God." After hearing Tauler preach six times, Nicholas sought an interview with the preacher.

"Master Tauler," he said "you must die!" "Die," said the popular Strasburg preacher, "What do you mean?" The next day Nicholas came again and said, "John Tauler, you must die to live." What do you mean?" said Tauler. "Get alone with God," said Nicholas, "leave your crowded church, your admiring congregation, your hold on this city. Get aside to your cell, be alone and you will see what I mean."

His plain speaking at first offended Tauler, and his resentment only proved how accurate the diagnosis at which Nicholas had arrived was.

Tauler was a long time coming to the end of himself, but in Nicholas he had a patient and loving teacher. The process of 'breaking' was slow and painful, but when God is working for eternity, He takes account of no time, nor does He spare His servants any humiliation or suffering, if only they may be made vessels broken and empty, "for the Master's use made meet."

Tauler felt himself obliged to obey the advice of his friend. He left his church, fled from popularity, was accounted crazy by his friends, and , alone with God, fought the greatest of all battles - the battle with the hydra-headed monster, self. Assaulted by Satan, despairing of his own heart, overcome with weakness of body, broken-hearted on account of his sins, his wasted time and lost opportunities, he lay in his room, weak and stricken down with sorrow. Then John Tauler died, and heard a voice speaking to him and saying: "Trust in God and be at peace, and know that when He was on earth as a man, He made the sick whom He healed in body, sound also in the soul."

Thus John Tauler rose from the dead. When he came to himself, after not knowing how or where he was, he was filled with a new strength and might in all his being, and the things which for a time were dark to him, were now bright and clear. The pathway of dying to

his reputation,

his strength,

his wisdom,

his zeal,

his eloquence

had been a long and painful one. He had been treading the rugged road of complete self-abnegation for two whole years, while everyone who knew him wondered what had become of him, and what was the reason for his long silence.

Tauler sent for Nicholas, who said, when he learnt of his friend's experiences: "Now, thou art a partaker of the grace of God. Now, thou wilt understand the Scriptures, and be able to show thy fellow Christians the Way to Eternal Life. Now, one of thy sermons will bring more fruit than a hundred aforetime."

— FROM THE BOOK, "BEYOND HUMILIATION" BY GLEGORY MANTLE

The Psalmist proclaimed,

"Lord, who may dwell in your sanctuary?
Who may live on your holy hill?

*He whose walk is blameless
And who does what is righteous,
who speaks the truth from his heart
And has no slander on his tongue,
who does his neighbour no wrong
and casts no slur on his fellow-man,
who despises a vile man
but honours those who fear the Lord,
who keeps his oath even when it hurts»*
(Psalm 15: 1-4).

6

WAITING ON GOD IN PRAYER SO AS TO KNOW GOD'S WILL

"This is the confidence we have in approaching God: that if we ask anything according to his will, he hears us. And if we know that he hears us - whatever we ask - we know that we have what we asked of him" (1John 5:14-15)

"For my thoughts are not your thoughts, neither are your ways my ways," declares the Lord
. "As the heavens are higher than the earth, so are my ways higher than your ways and my thoughts than your thoughts" (Isaiah 55: 8-9)

True prayer begins in the heart of God, for true prayer has as its goal the execution of God's will. God could execute His will unaided by man. However, He has decided to make man His co-worker and thus have him participate in the execution of the divine will.

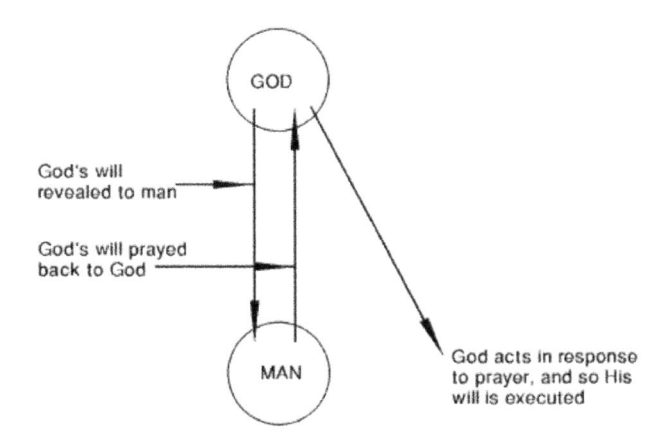

WHAT TAKES PLACE DURING PRAYER

Any praying that is not according to the will of God is a waste of time. God only hears us if we ask according to His will. All asking that conflicts with His will will go unheard by Him. There may be no sin between the believer and God. However, if the believer makes a request that is not according to God's will, and prays it unceasingly to God, he will nevertheless go away unheard because he did not pray according to the will of God.

There are many saints who make prayer a gamble. They say that they will just present many things to God and allow God to decide which are His will and answer them while throwing away what is not God's will. This is a very infantile attitude. It cannot lead to real praying; for there is no certainty about the issues involved. There are others who think that God can be moved by their prayers to give them anything they want, provided they insist in prayer. Again, this is great folly; for, to want what God has not willed for you to have is disaster.

God's will, God's thoughts and God's ways for every child of His are a billion times better than the best will, the best thoughts and the best ways that any child of His can ever conceive for himself. God's will, God's thoughts and God's ways are heavenly in origin, purpose and direction. The best will, thoughts and ways of man are earthly in origin, purpose and direction. The difference is enormous. Let us try to illustrate it:

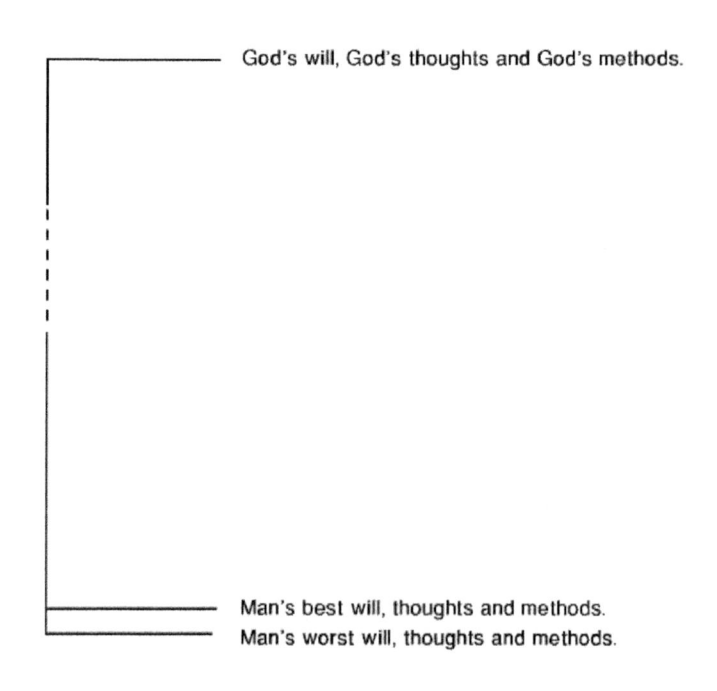

```
|―――――――― God's will, God's thoughts and God's methods.
|
|
|
|
|
|
|
|
|
|
|
|
|―――――――― Man's best will, thoughts and methods.
―――――――――  Man's worst will, thoughts and methods.
```

One of the most terrible things that the Enemy did with the fall was that he sowed into man a deep suspicion of God. Many people, including God's children, fear that God may not have the best in store for them. They think they have better plans, methods and all else for themselves than what God has. Consequently, they fear God's will and labour to run away from it as much as possible. We judge this deceit of the enemy and testify that God has the best in store for His children. The Bible says ,

> "Which of you, if his son asks for bread, will give him a stone? Or if he asks for a fish, will give him a snake? If you, then, though you are evil, know how to give good gifts to your children, how much more will your Father in heaven give good gifts to those who ask him!" (Matthew 7:9-11).

You may need to be assured that God loves you. God loves you to the same extent to which He loves the Lord Jesus. The Lord Jesus prayed,

> "May they be brought to complete unity to let the world know that you sent me and <u>have loved them even as you have loved me</u>" (John 17:23).

Again the Lord Jesus prayed,

> " I have made you known to them, and will continue to make you known in order <u>that the love you have for me may be in them</u> and that I myself may be in them" (John 17:26)

God's will is the best for you. God's thoughts are the best for you. God's methods are the best for you. This being so, an important part of prayer is to wait on God and empty ourselves of our own thoughts, will and method, to seek, find and know His own will, thoughts and methods, thirdly, to make His thoughts, will and methods ours, and then to pray to Him that His thoughts, will and methods which have now become ours be executed.

Waiting in prayer then has four purposes :

1. *To enable me to see that my will is not for my best interest.*

2. *To enable me to see that His will is for my best interest.*
3. *To enable me to throw away my will.*
4. *To enable me to make His will mine.*

REVELATION OF THE FACT THAT ONE'S OWN WILL IS NOT FOR ONE'S BEST INTEREST.

Although one's own will is not for one's best interest, it may not be so obvious. For those who know the Lord and walk with Him, this knowledge is obvious. For others, it needs to be revealed to them.

The believer will come before the Lord and wait before Him in prayer. He will then plead with God to write it on his heart, what he knows in the head, that his will is not to his best interest. As the believer waits thus before the Lord, a revelation will be communicated to his spirit on the dangers of his own will.

As the believer continues to wait before the Lord, the Holy Spirit will reveal to him the glorious beauty of God's will for him and the fact that all that God has designed for him is for his own good in time and eternity.

As he waits further before the Lord, he will pray and receive power from the Lord to uproot his own will from his heart in a total way.

Finally, before the Lord, he will receive strength to enthrone God's will on his heart and power to love that will and to desire its fulfilment with the whole of his being.

As the believer waits before God, he may be filled with the Holy Spirit and thus be aflame with great zeal to see God's will accomplished as soon as possible to His greatest satisfaction.

We write, from hard-earned experience, that it is near impossible to wait before the Lord in prayer honestly presenting your will, your thoughts and your methods before Him for examination and correction, and not see all that has its origin in self exposed for what it is. We confess that with sustained waiting before God for one, two, three, four, five, six or seven days in a shut-in retreat, one has come out aflame for the Lord and for His will. We also confess that the folly of one's will has been made more obvious with increasing time in His presence, which we can represent as follows:

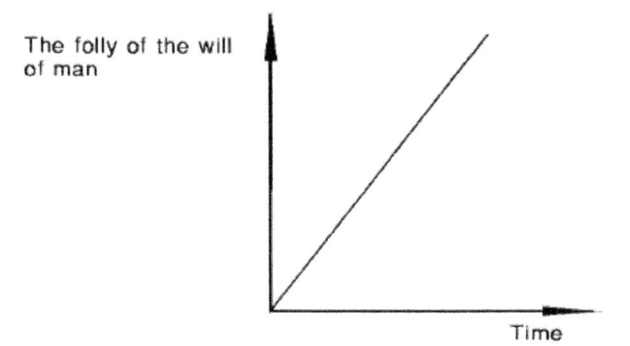

The folly of the will of man is more obvious as one waits increasingly before God.

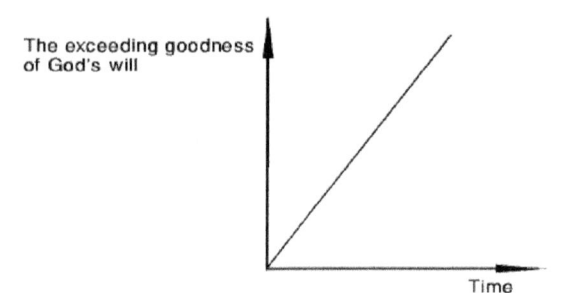

The exceeding goodness of God's will becomes more obvious as one waits increasingly before Him.

WAITING BEFORE GOD IN PRAYER AS A WAY TO KNOWING GOD'S WILL

THE EXAMPLE OF MOSES - 1

«The daughters of Zelophehad son of Hepher, the son of Gilead, the son of Machir, the son of Manassseh, belonged to the clans of Manasseh son of Joseph. The names of the daughters were Mahlah, Noah, Hoglah, Milcah and Tirzah. They approached the entrance to the Tent of Meeting and stood before Moses, Eleazar the priest, the leaders and the whole assembly, and said, "Our father died in the desert. He was not among Korah's followers, who banded together against the Lord, but he died for his own sins and left no sons. Why should our father's name disappear from his clan because he had no son? Give us property among our father's relatives."

So Moses brought their case before the Lord and the Lord said to him,

"What Zelophehad's daughters are saying is right. You

must certainly give them property as an inheritance among their father's relatives and give their father's inheritance over to them"(Numbers 27:1-7).

Moses was presented with a situation he did not know how to handle. He brought the matter up to the Lord. He waited before the Lord and the Lord spoke back to him. He then had God's will on the matter which he executed.

THE EXAMPLE OF MOSES - 2

While the Israelites were in the desert , a man was found gathering wood on the Sabbath day. Those who found him gathering wood brought him to Moses and Aaron and the whole assembly, and they kept him in custody, because it was not clear what should be done to him. Then the Lord said to Moses,

> "The man must die. The whole assembly must stone him outside the camp." So the assembly took him outside the camp and stoned him to death, as the Lord commanded Moses»(Numbers 15: 32-36).

Again there was a new situation in which Moses did not know God's will. He did not act on his imagination. He presented the situation to God, kept the man in custody and waited. God spoke and thus he knew what God's will was and thus he executed it. Moses thus put aside his will and sought God's will. Hallelujah!

THE EXAMPLE OF MOSES - 3

«The Lord spoke to Moses in the Desert of Sinai in the first month of the second year after they had come out of Egypt. He said, 'Make the Israelites celebrate the Passover at the appointed time. Celebrate it at the appointed time, at twilight on the fourteenth day of the first month, in accordance with all its rules and regulations.'

So Moses told the Israelites to celebrate the Passover, and they did so on the fourteenth day of the first month. The Israelites did everything just as the Lord commanded Moses. But some of them could not celebrate the Passover on that day because they were ceremonially unclean on account of a dead body. So they came to Moses and Aaron the same day and said to Moses, 'We have become unclean because of a dead body, but why should we be kept from presenting the Lord's offering with the other Israelites at the appointed time?'

Moses answered them, 'Wait until I find out what the Lord commands concerning you.'

Then the Lord said to Moses,

> "Tell the Israelites: 'When any of you or your descendants are unclean because of a dead body or are away on a journey, they may still celebrate the Lord's Passover. They are to celebrate it on the fourteenth day of the second month at twilight. They are to eat the lamb, together with unleavened bread and bitter herbs. They must not leave any of it till morning or break any of its bones. When they celebrate the Passover, they must follow all the regulations. But if a man who is ceremonially clean and not on a journey fails to celebrate the Passover, that person must be cut off

from his people because he did not present the Lord's offering at the appointed time. That man will bear the consequences of his sins"(Numbers 9: 1-13).

Again a matter was raised about which Moses did not know the will of God. He answered the people, "Wait until I find out what the Lord commands concerning you." They waited while Moses took the matter before God. Moses presented the matter to God in prayer and waited for God to speak back to him. How long he waited before God, we do not know. We only know that he waited until God answered. When God answered, the period of waiting ended.

THE EXAMPLE OF JOSHUA - 1

"But the Israelites acted unfaithfully with regards to the devoted things; Achan son of Carmi, the son of Zimri, the son of Zerah, of the tribe of Judah, took some of them. So the Lord's anger burnt against Israel. Now Joshua sent men from Jericho to Ai, which is near Beth Aven to the East of Bethel, and told them, 'Go up and spy out the region.' So the men went out and spied out Ai.

When they returned to Joshua, they said, 'Not all the people will have to go up against Ai. Send two or three thousand men to take it and do not weary all the people, for only a few men are there.' So about three thousand men went up; but they were routed by the men of Ai, who killed about thirty-six of them. They chased the Israelites from the city gates as far as the stone quarries and struck them down on the slopes. At this the heart of the people melted and became like water.

Then Joshua tore his clothes and fell face down to the ground before the ark of the Lord, remaining there till evening. The elders of Israel did the same, and sprinkled dust on their heads. And Joshua said, 'Ah, Sovereign Lord, why did you ever bring this people across the Jordan to deliver us into the hands of the Amorites to destroy us? If only we had been content to stay on the other side of the Jordan! O Lord, what can I say, now that Israel has been routed by its enemies? The Canaanites and the other people of the country will hear about this and they will surround us and wipe out our name from the earth. What then will you do for your own great name?'

The Lord said to Joshua,

'Stand up! What are you doing down on your face? Israel has sinned; they have violated my covenant, which I commanded them to keep. They have taken some of the devoted things; they have stolen, they have lied, they have put them with their own possessions. That is why the Israelites cannot stand against their enemies; they turn their backs and run because they have been made liable to destruction. I will not be with you any more unless you destroy whatever among you is devoted to destruction'" (Joshua 7:1-12).

The initial attack on Ai failed. Joshua and the elders went before the Lord and waited before Him till evening. Then Joshua presented his problem to God and God answered, revealing to him why things had gone the way they had gone, and how things were to be corrected.. Had he not waited before the Lord, he would not have known what was wrong and what to do about it. Those who seek God's face and present their problems to Him, and wait for His answer, grow in a knowledge of Him and His ways. Those who handle their problems themselves grow in ignorance and confusion.

THE EXAMPLE OF JOSHUA - 2

Now when all the kings west of the Jordan heard about these things - there in the hill country, in the western foothills and along the entire coast of the Great Sea as far as Lebanon (Kings of the Hittites, Amorites, Canaanites, Perizzites, Hevites and Jebusites) - they came together to make war against Joshua and Israel.

However, when the people of Gibeon heard what Joshua had done to Jericho and Ai, they resorted to a ruse: They went as a delegation whose donkeys were loaded with worn-out sacks and old wineskins, cracked and mended. The men put worn and patched sandals on their feet and wore old clothes . All the bread of their food supply was dry and mouldy. Then they went to Joshua in the camp at Gilgal and said to him and the men of Israel, "We have come from a distant country; make a treaty with us."

The men of Israel said to the Hivites, "But perhaps you live near us. How then can we make a treaty with you?" "We are your servants," they said to Joshua. But Joshua asked, " Who are you and where do you come from?"

They answered: "Your servants have come from a very distant country because of the fame of the Lord your God. For we have heard reports of him: all that he did in Egypt , and all that he did to the two kings of the Amorites east of the Jordan-Sihon king of Heshbon, and Og, king of Bashan, who reigned in Ashtaroth. And our elders and all those living in our country said to us, " Take provisions for your journey, go and meet them and say to them, "We are your servants; make a treaty with us." This bread of ours was warm when we parked it at home on the day we left to come to you. But now see how dry and mouldy it is. And these wineskins that we filled were new but see how cracked they are. And our clothes and sandals are worn out by the very long journey."

<u>The men of Israel sampled their provisions but did not enquire of the Lord</u>. Then Joshua made a treaty of peace with them to let them live, and the leaders of the assembly ratified it by oath.

Three days after they made the treaty with the Gibeonites, the Israelites heard that they were neighbours, living near them. So the Israelites set out and on the third day came to their cities: Gibeon, Kephirah, Beeroth and Kiriath Jearim. But the Israelites did not attack them because the leaders of the assembly had sworn an oath to them by the Lord, the God of Israel.

The whole assembly grumbled against the leaders, but all the leaders answered,

"We have given them our oath by the Lord, the God of Israel, and we cannot touch them now. This is what we will do to them: we will let them live, so that wrath will not fall on us for breaking the oath we swore to them" (Joshua 9:1-20).

Joshua and the leaders faced a decision. They could have waited on the Lord to hear what he would say. Unfortunately, they did not turn to the Lord. Thy did not wait on Him.

They did not seek His face. They did not enquire of Him. They trusted in their own judgment. They sampled their provisions. They based their judgment on what they could see. They did not base it on the Lord, and they were absolutely mistaken.

Every believer has the choice between turning to the Lord and waiting on Him in prayer to receive guidance and instruction, or turning to himself,

1. *reasoning,*
2. *analyzing,*
3. *synthesizing and*
4. *deciding.*

The results of the two processes are as far apart as heaven is from the earth.

As you can see, the question is: "Do we want to turn to the Lord or do we want to turn to ourselves?"

If we decide to turn to the Lord, we have to get in tune with Him. All that stands in the way will have to be removed. We will have to come and be prepared to wait before Him as long as it will take for Him to speak. Often, He will remain silent until we are desperate to hear Him. Sometimes He will not speak until we have come to the end of hearing our own voices. When we have come to the end of hearing our own voices and are truly open to hear His voice, He will speak. It may take

1. *one hour,*
2. *twelve hours,*
3. *twenty-four hours,*
4. *thirty-six hours,*

5. *forty-eight hours,*
6. *etc.*

It may take

1. *seven days,*
2. *ten days,*
3. *fourteen days,*
4. *twenty one days,*
5. *etc.*

The important thing is not how long it will take for Him to speak. The important thing is that He will speak to the one who has decided that he will not go away unless he has heard God. Those who have their own answers to fall on, should the Lord not speak, cannot wait until He speaks.

Waiting on God in prayer is for people who have made God their all and His will the only will they will know. One such person wrote :

> «*My soul finds rest in God alone;*
> *my salvation comes from him.*
> *He alone is my rock and my salvation;*
> *he is my fortress, I shall never be shaken*»
> (Psalm 62: 1-2)
> «*Find rest, O my soul, in God alone;*
> *my hope comes from him.*
> *He alone is my rock and my salvation;*
> *he is my fortress, I shall not be shaken"*
> (Psalm 62: 5-6).

THE EXAMPLE OF DAVID - 1

When David was told,

> "Look, the Philistines are fighting against Keilah and are looting the threshing-floors," he enquired of the Lord, saying, "Shall I go and attack these Philistines?" The Lord answered him, "Go, attack the Philistines and save Keilah." But David's men said to him, "Here in Judah we are afraid. How much more, then, if we go to Keilah against the Philistine forces!"
>
> Once again David enquired of the Lord, and the Lord answered him, "Go down to Keilah, for I am going to give the Philistines into your hand." So David and his men went to Keilah, fought the Philistines and carried off their livestock. He inflicted heavy losses on the Philistines and saved the people of Keilah» (I Samuel 23: 1-5).

David enquired of the Lord and the Lord spoke to him. His people resisted what he had received from the Lord. He enquired of the Lord again. The Lord confirmed what He had told him. He obeyed the Lord and won the battle.

THE EXAMPLE OF DAVID - 2

In the course of time, David enquired of the Lord.

> "Shall I go up to one of the towns of Judah?" he asked. The Lord said, "Go up." David asked, "Where shall I go?" "To Hebron," the Lord answered. So David went up there with his two wives, Ahinoam of Jezreel and Abigail, the widow of Nabal of Carmel. David also took the men who were with him, each with his family, and they settled in Hebron and its

towns. Then the men of Judah came to Hebron and there they anointed David King over the house of Judah» (2 Samuel 2 : 1-4).

David sought the Lord and the Lord revealed to Him what he was to do. Then he did it!

THE EXAMPLE OF DAVID - 3

"During the reign of David, there was a famine for three successive years; so David sought the face of the Lord. The Lord said, 'It is on account of Saul and his blood-stained house, it is because he put the Gibeonites to death.'

The king summoned the Gibeonites and spoke to them. (Now the Gibeonites were not a part of Israel but were survivors of the Amorites; the Israelites had sworn to spare them, but Saul in his zeal for Israel and for Judah had tried to annihilate them.) David asked the Gibeonites, 'What shall I do for you? How shall I make amends so that you will bless the Lord's inheritance?'

The Gibeonites answered him, 'We have no right to demand gold or silver from Saul or his family, nor do we have the right to put anyone in Israel to death.'

'What do you want me to do for you?' David asked. They answered the king, 'As for the man who destroyed us and plotted against us so that we have been decimated and have no place in Israel, let seven of his male descendants be given to us to be killed and exposed before the Lord at Gibeah of Saul - the Lord's chosen one.' So the king said, 'I will give them to you.'

The king spared Mephibosheth the son of Jonathan, the son of Saul, because of the oath before the Lord between David and Jonathan of Saul. But the king took Armoni and Mephibosheth, the two sons of Aiah's daughter Rizpah, whom she had borne to Saul, together with the five sons of Saul's daughter Merab, whom she had borne to Adriel son of Barzillai the Meholathite. He handed them over to the Gibeonites, who killed and exposed them on a hill before the Lord. All seven of them fell together; they were put to death during the first days of the harvest, just as the barley harvest was beginning. After that God answered prayer on behalf of the land" (2 Samuel 21: 1-14).

There was famine for three successive years. Some would have said, "Well, it is a natural process." David did not say that. He knew that the Lord reigns over

1. *the universe,*
2. *the people,*
3. *the animals,*
4. *the climate,*
5. *the winds,*
6. *the productivity,*
7. *etc.*

Consequently, he sought the face of the Lord. Of course, David sought the face of the Lord daily in his ordinary communion with the Lord. He testified,

"O Lord, in the morning you hear my voice; in the morning I lay my requests before you and wait in expectation" (Psalm 5:3).

However, this was a special seeking of the Lord in order to know where the problem was. He wanted to know God's mind on the matter. So he took the matter to God and waited before the Lord for an answer. How long did he wait before the Lord? We do not know. We however know that he waited until the Lord spoke. Then he had God's mind of the matter and acted on the revelation that he received from the Lord.

We insist that those who wait on the Lord should keep waiting until He speaks. It is useless to come before Him and go away before He has spoken to you.

THE EXAMPLE OF REBEKAH

Isaac prayed to the Lord on behalf of his wife, because she was barren. The Lord answered his prayer, and his wife Rebekah became pregnant. The babies jostled each other within her, and she said,

> "Why is this happening to me?" So she went to enquire of the Lord. The Lord said to her, "Two nations are in your womb, and two peoples from within you will be separate; one people will be stronger than the other, and the older will serve the younger" (Genesis 25 :21-23).

If Rebekah had not been spiritually sensitive, she would have ignored the jostling of the babies within her. She would then not have sought the Lord. She would consequently have missed the critical information which the Lord gave her when she went to enquire of Him.

Have there not been situations in which you ought to have withdrawn and enquired of the Lord? Did you withdraw and wait before Him in prayer?

These people sought God and He revealed His will to them and they did it. They were prepared to go into His presence and to wait until He spoke. This is a great need for the saints today. There is a lot of confusion because the saints would not wait, wait and wait, wait and wait before the Lord in prayer until He speaks to them.

Will you do something about it?

❼
WAITING ON GOD INSTEAD OF TURNING TO MAN

The following extract from a biography of a servant of the Lord might help you to come to grips with what we are labouring to communicate.

When Mr Howells returned from Keswick, Mr Edwards made him a definite offer of Glynderwen for £6,300. "I thought he would have asked for more than that," said Mr. Howells, and meant to accept his offer; but the Lord said, «No ! It was a talent of gold I promised you -£6,150, and not a penny more." I stood against God in a second, I showed my attitude towards Him, but He didn't say another word, and I knew I wouldn't dare disobey Him. When I questioned the price, Mr. Edwards told me to discuss the matter with his solicitor the next day. But instead I went to a friend's house in Llanelly, where for two days I neither ate nor drank. What agony I went through, but what lessons I learnt! I told God that He had called me to fight the church of -- and here he was quibbling over £150; but he turned it back on me. Hadn't I claimed Glynderwen for Him? Didn't I believe then that the -- wouldn't get it? If the battle had been won in Scotland, could the Holy Spirit ever allow Mr Edwards to sell the property to anyone else? I was beginning to get strong now. Was Mr. Edwards in the hands of the Holy Spirit? Could the devil induce him to sell it? During the two days I came right through, and what liberty I had! Whatever price the enemy offered, he could never get it. I had heard that Mr. Edwards was a great businessman, but I had to learn that God could control him. I came to the place where I knew that whenever God wants to take over a property, the owner has very little to do with it.

"*When I returned home, I received a letter from Mr. Edwards saying that all negotiations were off. As I had not gone to the solicitor, I had proved that I was not a businessman, and he would sell to the other people, who were offering him £10,000.*

I was not affected by the letter because the Unseen Captain had taken over, and the responsibility was not mine any longer. I wrote Mr. Edwards and told him quite plainly that it was much harder for me to refuse his offer of £6,300 than to accept it, but God had said I was not to go above £6,150, and after spending two days with Him neither eating nor drinking, He had confirmed His word to me. I had a letter by return saying he would drop the £500! He refused to make a single penny on it. Wasn't that God?"

When the agreement had been signed, Mr. Howells had ten days in which to pay the deposit. On the day he was due to go to the solicitor with the money, he was £140 short. He was still this sum short when the actual hour arrived, so in faith, he set off to the office without it. He hadn't been there long when Mrs. Howells arrived. She had followed him down with the post, and in it were three cheques, which made up the £140 to the penny.

But the real battle came over the real sum to be paid. He had never dealt in large amounts before, and the burden was great upon him. He was to take no meetings nor make any appeals. His eyes went on God alone. He gave himself to prayer, spending his days in his little upstair bedroom in his mother's home, alone with God and His word from 6 a.m. to 5 p.m., when he took his first meal. In the evenings he continued in prayer with his newly found prayer partner, Mr Tommy Howells. Ten months were spent in this way until the victory was complete.

Below is how the victory was completed: The next sum asked for was £2,000. The Lord sent gifts varying from 5s to £300 during the next three months, but when he still only had £1700, the solicitor suddenly called for it to be paid by eleven o'clock the next morning. At first he was baffled a bit, as to why the Lord had allowed this sudden demand to be made. He was walking down Wind Street in Swansea, and as he came under the bridge, the word came to him, "Trust ye in the Lord for ever, for in the Lord Jehovah are everlasting resources." It was a word from heaven to him, and he believed that by eleven o'clock the next morning, he would be passing back under that bridge having the money with him. He had a train to catch, and finding an empty carriage, he got down on his knees and praised the Lord. He could have danced for joy, he said. The next morning he had the £300. The woman who sent it told him afterwards that she had a very great burden for him during the very-half hour that he believed. It was so heavy on her that she had to close her shop and post the money off to him. He was able to pay the £2000 that day and have £18 to the good!

> — FROM REES HOWELLS INTERCESSOR
> «BY NORMAN GRUBB, LUTTERWORTH
> PRESS. LONDON 1981

Do you see the price he paid. He was not to take meetings at which he could share his needs. He could make no appeals. His eyes went on God alone. He had to deal with God and deal with God and deal with God!

He spent the time between 6.a.m and 5.p.m, eleven hours alone with God for ten months!!! It was no hurried affair. He had to exert himself. Can you imagine eleven hours of praying everyday for eleven months for just one issue?

And he fasted for the ten months! His first meal was after 5.p.m. And that was not all. In the evening he continued to pray with his prayer partner on the issue.

God could have brought deliverance after the first hour of his praying. Why did He not do it? I think the answer lies in what waiting on God in prayer does to the one who waits. Waiting transforms the waiting person into the likeness of God. The degree of transformation seems to be proportional to the time spent before God.

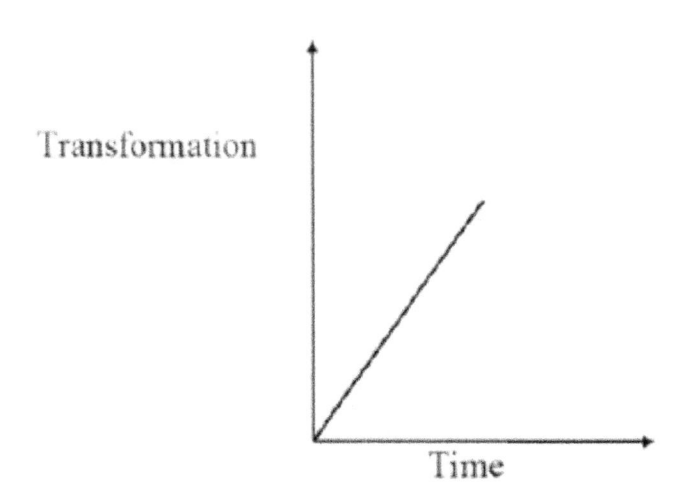

If the person is one that God wants to use only for a short time, He may grant his requests in a relatively short time so that the person can go away. However, for the person whom God wants to use for a sustained time, God is not just interested in supplying his needs. God is interested in the person and God wants to build a relationship with the person. Because God wants to build a quality relationship with him, He will keep him in His presence for as long as possible; so that the person will not only have his needs met, but he will put on God. We know that how much of God a person has put on is directly proportional to the amount of time invested in being in God's presence. We can represent it graphically as follows.

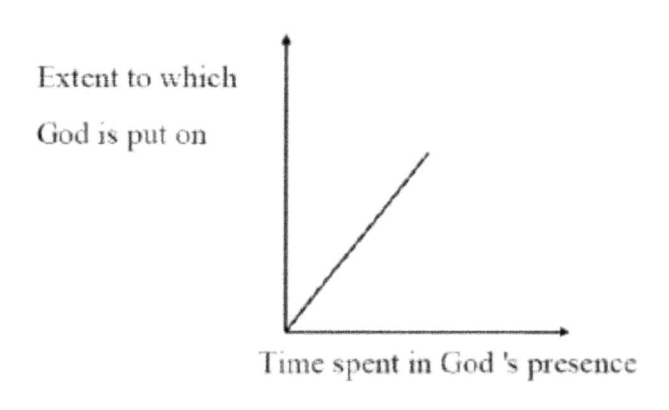

Extent to which God is put on

Time spent in God's presence

Rees Howells did not only receive the money after the ten months of spending eleven hours with God alone. He put on God and, consequently, grew spiritually into the man who could run the school the way God wanted. If he had obtained the money after investing less time with God, he might have lacked some of the character traits that were needed to hold the school for God.

The Psalmist proclaimed:

«*Wait for the Lord and keep his way. He will exalt you to*

inherit the land; When the wicked are cut off, you will see it. I have seen a wicked and ruthless man flourish like a green tree in its native soil, but he soon passed away and was no more; though I looked for him, he could not be found» (Psalm 37: 34-36).

8

WAITING ON THE LORD IN PRAYER: THE EXAMPLE OF MOSES ON THE MOUNTAIN - 1

Then he said to Moses, "Come up to the Lord, you and Aaron, Nadab and Abihu, and seventy of the elders of Israel. You are to worship at a distance, but Moses alone is to approach the Lord; the others must not come near. And the people may not come up with him."
When Moses went and told the people all the Lord's words and laws, they responded with one voice,
"Everything the Lord has said we will do." Moses then wrote down everything the Lord had said.
«He got up early the next morning and built an altar at the foot of the mountain and set up twelve stone pillars representing the twelve tribes of Israel. Then he sent young Israelite men, and they offered burnt offerings to the Lord. Moses took half of the blood and put it in bowls and the other half he sprinkled on the altar. Then he took the Book of the Covenant and read it to the people. They responded, "We will do everything the Lord has said; we will obey."

Moses then took the blood, sprinkled it at the people and said, "This is the blood of the covenant that the Lord has made with you in accordance with all these words."

Moses and Aaron, Nadab and Abihu, and the seventy elders of Israel went up and saw the God of Israel. Under his feet was something like a pavement made of sapphire, clear as the sky itself. But God did not raise his hand against these leaders of the Israelites; they saw God, and they ate and drank.

The Lord said to Moses, "Come up to me on the mountain and stay here, and I will give you the tablets of stone, with the law and commandments I have written for their instruction."

Then Moses set out with Joshua his assistant, and Moses went up on the mountain of God. He said to the elders, "Wait here for us until we come back to you. Aaron and Hur are with you, and anyone involved in a dispute can go to them."

When Moses went up on the mountain, the cloud covered it, and the glory of the Lord settled on Mount Sinai. For six days the cloud covered the mountain, and on the seventh day the Lord called to Moses from within the cloud. To the Israelites the glory of the Lord looked like a consuming fire on top of the mountain. Then Moses entered the cloud as he went on up the mountain. And he stayed on the mountain forty days and forty nights.

The Lord said to Moses, "Tell the Israelites to bring me an offering. You are to receive the offering for me from each man whose heart prompts him to give. These are the offerings you are to receive from them: gold, silver and bronze; blue, purple and scarlet yarn and fine linen; goat hair; ram skin dyed red and hides of sea cows; acacia wood; olive oil for the light; spices for the anointing oil and for the fragrant incense; and onyx stones and other gems to be mounted on the ephod and breastpiece.

Then have them make a sanctuary for me, and I will dwell among them. Make this tabernacle and all its furnishings exactly like the pattern I will show you. When the Lord finished speaking to Moses on Mount Sinai, he gave him the two tablets of the Testimony, the tablets of stone inscribed by the finger of God" (Exodus 24:1-8; 25:1-9; 31:18).

Moses, Aaron, Abihu and seventy of the elders of Israel were invited by the Lord to come up to Him. It was a wonderful invitation. They went up and saw the God of Israel. Under His feet was something like a pavement made of sapphire; clear as the sky itself. God did not raise His hand against these leaders of the Israelites; they saw God, and they ate and drank.

These people went as far as they could. They saw what they could see. It was so much for them. They celebrated - they ate and drank. They had no desire to go further. They were satisfied with what they had seen of God.

There is a sense in which God will allow a man to see what he wants to see of Him. There is a sense in which God gives a man what he, the man, wants.

- *Those who want nothing of God are given nothing of God.*
- *Those who want a little of God are given a little of God.*
- *Those who want much of God are given much of God.*
- *It is true that you know God as much as you want to know Him.*

- *It is true that you have God as much as you want to have Him.*
- *It is true that you are related to God as much as you want to be related to Him.*

The Lord said,

> "I love those who love me, and those who seek me find me"(Proverbs 8:17).

Even those who seek Him are in classes, in grades. Some seek Him to a small extent. Others seek Him to an average extent. Others seek Him to an above average extent. Others seek Him with all their hearts, all their souls and all their bodies. He is found to the extent to which He is sought. The extent to which He is found is directly proportional to the extent to which He is sought.

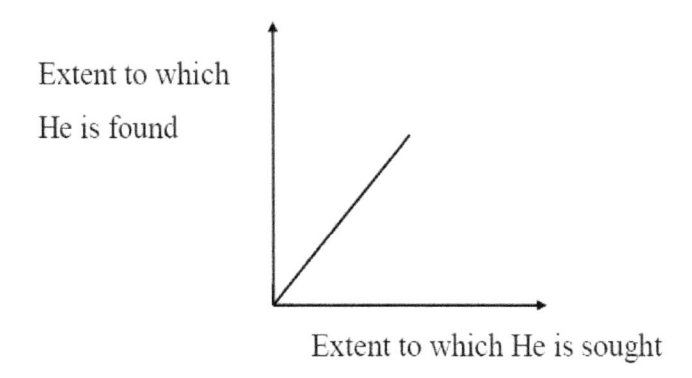

Another way of looking at the issue is to say that Moses had things to transact with God that the others did not need to enter into. This is a most important point. People wait before the Lord in prayer depending on what they want to transact with Him. Those who have no business to transact with Him will not bother to wait on Him in prayer. To these, waiting on Him is a waste of time. Those who have some small issues to treat with Him can do so during their normal times of encounter with Him. Those who have major issues to settle with Him wait before Him because the issues cannot be handled in the small periods that are available for daily intercourse with Him. These then seek Him and wait before Him, and will not go away until they encounter Him and receive His solution to their problems.

We can therefore say that the extent to which a person is prepared to wait before the Lord is directly proportional to the problem that he wants to settle with God. We can present it as follows:

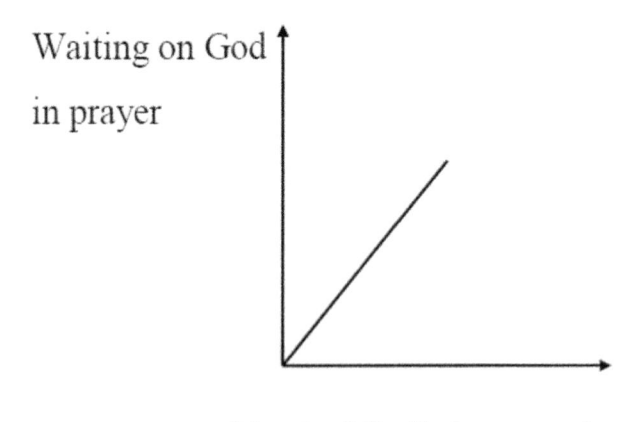

Waiting on God in prayer

Need of God's intervention

However, this is not all. There are people with enormous needs which ought to compel them to wait before the Lord. However, they would not seek Him because they do not want to pay the price that must be paid to seek Him. If they could have the Lord intervene and solve their problems at no cost to them, they would gladly have the solutions He offers. However, to have Him solve their problems after they have waited on Him and encountered Him, is a price that they do not want to pay. They know that there are sacrifices that must be made to wait on Him in prayer. Sin will have to be sacrificed; self-will will have to be sacrificed; confessions will have to be made and restitutions will have to be carried out. Because of this price that has to be paid, many who have problems that require waiting on Him for solutions, nevertheless avoid waiting on Him. We can conclude that the willingness to wait before the Lord is directly proportional to the willingness to pay the price for encountering Him. We again present it as follows:

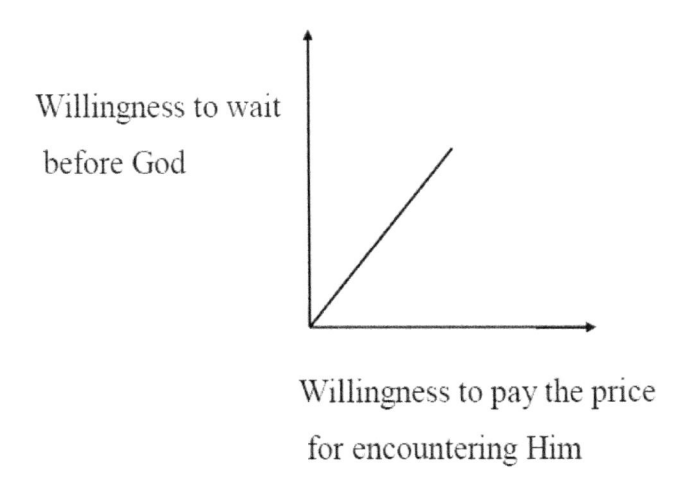

Willingness to wait before God

Willingness to pay the price for encountering Him

SIX DAYS OF WAITING FOR MOSES

The Bible says,

> "When Moses went up on the mountain, the cloud covered it, and the glory of the Lord settled on

Mount Sinai. For six days the cloud covered the
mountain, and on the seventh day the Lord called
to Moses from within the cloud" (Exodus 24:15-16).

Moses was on the mountain. One could have thought that God would immediately begin to talk to him! The cloud covered the mountain! The glory of the Lord settled on Mount Sinai! God was there and God was ready! Why did God not begin to speak to Moses?

Our suggestion is that although all was ready on God's part (and God is always ready), Moses was not ready. Moses was physically there, but Moses was not spiritually ready to enter into intercourse with God. Why was this so?

It was so because Moses had to examine himself. The cloud was there. The glory of the Lord was there and the Lord was there. In God's immediate presence, Moses could see himself as he could not see himself before, and perhaps needed to deeply repent:

Job justified himself fully. He said,

> "I have made a covenant with my eyes not to look
> lustfully at a girl...... If I have walked in falsehood
> or my foot has hurried after deceit - let God weigh
> me in honest scales and he will know that I am
> blameless.... If my heart has been enticed by a
> woman.... If I have denied justice to my
> menservants and maidservants when they had a
> grievance against me...... If I have denied the
> desires of the poor or let the eyes of the widow
> grow weary...... If I have seen anyone perishing for
> lack of clothing, or a needy man without a garment
> and his heart did not bless me for warming him

> with the fleece from my sheep...... If I have put my trust in gold or said to pure gold, 'You are my security,'...... If I have rejoiced over my great wealth, the fortune my hands have gained..... If I have rejoiced at my enemy's misfortune or gloated over the trouble that came to him...... If I have concealed my sin as men do, by hiding my guilt in my heart because I so feared the crowd and so dreaded the contempt of the clans that I kept silent and would not go outside......" (Job 31:1-40).

Yes he justified himself in his own light and in the light that flowed from his friends. However, in God's presence he said,

> "My ears had heard of you but now my eyes have seen you. Therefore I despise myself and repent in dust and ashes" (Job 42:5-6).

The other thing is that, before Moses could begin to hear the voice of the Lord, he had to stop hearing the other voices - the voices of the Israelites, the voices of the Israelite leadership, the voices of his own mind and the voices of his own heart.

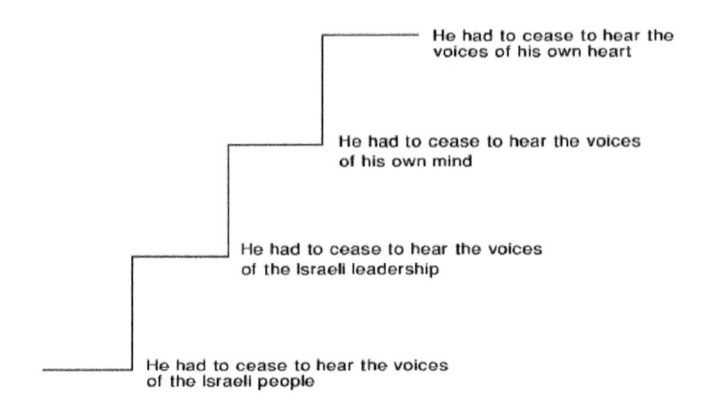

- He had to cease to hear the voices of his own heart
- He had to cease to hear the voices of his own mind
- He had to cease to hear the voices of the Israeli leadership
- He had to cease to hear the voices of the Israeli people

It possibly took six days for these voices to cease, and God patiently waited for them to cease before He started to speak.

Rees Howells said, "Although we may go away from the presence of people, how hard it is to silence the voice of self."

The voice of self can speak for

- one,
- two,
- three,
- four,
- five,
- six,
- seven,
- etc.

days. Those who go to wait on God in prayer should intercede that God should silence the voice of self so that they can listen to the voice of God.

It will often take active co-operation with the Holy Spirit for the voice of self to be silenced. If there are things to put right with God and man and, instead of doing something about it, there is prayer that the voice of self should cease, then this is self-deception. The voice will not cease. The waiting before God has already begun and the Holy Spirit is saying, "Go and put this matter right before more can be shown to you."

It may be that a person goes away to wait on God in prayer and when he gets to the place of waiting, he has to go back and put things right with someone or with some people before he comes back to the place of waiting. This will be in perfect order; for waiting in pretense is a waste of time. The Lord Jesus said,

> "Therefore, if you are offering your gift at the altar and there remember that your brother has something against you, leave your gift there in front of the altar. First go and be reconciled to your brother; then come and offer your gift" (Matthew 5:23-24).

FORTY DAYS AND FORTY NIGHTS OF LISTENING!

The problem of man is that he prefers to talk rather than to listen. Greatness is, in a sense, directly proportional to the power to listen. The greater the person, the greater his power to listen.

Greatness / The power to listen

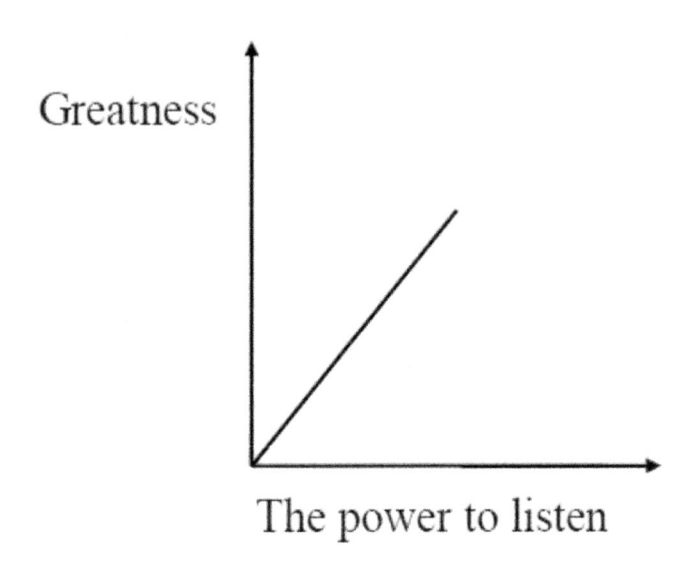

The small person cannot listen. He may not speak audibly, but he is speaking inside. It requires a fair degree of dying to self to be able to listen to another person. We say very certainly that the capacity to listen to another is directly proportional to the extent to which one has died to self.

```
         ^
The power |
to listen |        /
          |       /
          |      /
          |     /
          |    /
          |   /
          |  /
          | /
          |/_____>
             The extent to which
             one has died to self
```

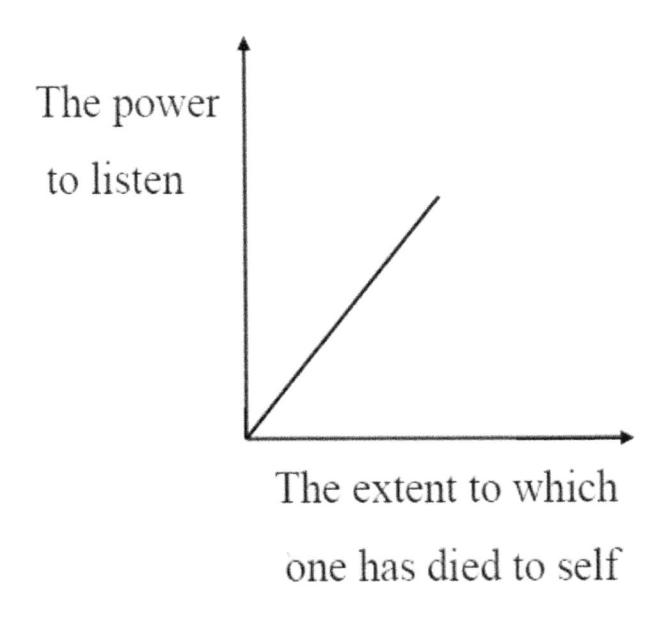

Instead of listening, many people are only waiting for you to say what you have to say so that they can take over and say what they have to say.

This may be another reason why Moses had to wait for six days, and was only called by the Lord from within the cloud on the seventh day. He had to learn to listen; for God was going to speak for long.

Could this be one of the main reasons why the saints are so underdeveloped in the spiritual science of waiting on God in prayer? Is the problem the fact that even after many years in the Lord, they are still babies in the "School of Listening to God" and, consequently, babies in the "School of Waiting On God in Prayer"?

Let me ask you a personal question, "Do you listen to man? Can someone speak to you for

- *15 minutes,*
- *30 minutes,*
- *60 minutes,*

and you just listen to him without drawing conclusions, saying something or wanting to say something? Have you learnt to silence your own thoughts,

- put away your preconceived ideas and listen,
- put away your desire to speak,
- put away your desire to be heard,

and given yourself away to listen to another?

The chances are that if you cannot listen to man, you are unlikely to listen to God. You may have to enroll in the School of Listening To Man and make some progress there before you enroll in the School of Listening To God.

CONCENTRATION

God began to speak to Moses, "Tell the children of Israel to bring me an offering...." It was critical that Moses should hear every word and remember everything that God was saying. He was not there in God's presence just to enjoy himself. He was not there for pleasure. He would have to tell the children of Israel exactly what God had said. He had to concentrate. Every word uttered by God was important.

God moved on and said,

"Then have them make a sanctuary for me......" Then

> He showed Moses a model of what it was to be like and insisted, "See that you make them according to the pattern shown you on the mountain" (Exodus 25:40)

. He showed Moses the altar of burnt offering and insisted,

> "Make the altar hollow, out of boards. It is to be made just as you were shown on the mountain" (Exodus 27:8).

Then He went on and on and gave Moses various instructions. It would seem that the first thing that the Lord did was to show Moses the heavenly model of what He wanted, and afterwards, He began to give him instructions insisting that things had to be done according to what had been shown him.

Moses stayed in God's presence until God finished speaking to him.

- *God decided how long the encounter was to be.*
- *God decided when to call Moses up.*
- *God decided for how long Moses was to wait.*
- *God decided when to call Moses into His presence.*
- *God decided what to say to Moses.*
- *God decided what to show Moses.*
- *God decided when Moses was to return.*
- *Glory be to His holy Name!*

CONSECRATION

The unconsecrated have nothing to wait on God for. If a person will not place all that he is and all that he has on the altar of God for all time, he is not serious about the Christian life and should not expect to have deep dealings with God.

Moses was shown much by God and told much by God. As he was coming down from the mountain, he must have had one pre-occupation - how to ensure that he obeyed all that God had told him.

That is the same attitude that all who wait on God in prayer should have. They should be people who fear the Lord and who will not take what He has shown them lightly.

We once went on a missionary journey that lasted 40 days. Brother Jean Ngankwe and I went to Kenya, Uganda, India, Israel, France and Spain preaching the Gospel in all these countries except in Israel. I had one burden during that journey. I wanted to know what the fear of the Lord was. I wanted the Lord to explain the fear of the Lord to me in terms that I could understand and relate to easily. Night after night, I raised the same question with Him, asking, "Father, what is the fear of the Lord?" It was in Spain on the 38th day of the trip, that the Lord spoke to me. He said to me, "The fear of the Lord, as far as you are concerned, implies that you obey everything the Lord has ever commanded you; that you keep every promise you have ever made to the Lord on your own." It was clear. It was settled. I prayed that the Holy Spirit should help me to remember all His commands to me and all my commitments to Him. I believe He did. I gathered them, wrote them out and got them typed. I am labouring to obey His commandments to me and to conform my acts to my words to Him. I have no choice in the matter.

To come to the Lord, seek Him, find Him, hear His voice and then go away to live as if He was not sought, not found and not heard is disaster indeed!

9

WAITING ON THE LORD IN PRAYER: THE EXAMPLE OF MOSES ON THE MOUNTAIN - 2

"When I went up on the mountain to receive the tablets of stone, the tablets of the covenant that the Lord had made with you, I stayed on the mountain forty days and forty nights; I ate no bread and drank no water. The Lord gave me two stone tablets inscribed by the finger of God. On them were all the commandments the Lord proclaimed to you on the mountain out of the fire, on the day of the assembly.

At the end of the forty days and forty nights, the Lord gave me the two stone tablets, the tablets of the covenant. Then the Lord told me, 'Go down from here at once, because, your people whom you brought out of Egypt have become corrupt. They have turned away quickly from what I commanded them and have made a cast idol for themselves.'

And the Lord said to me, 'I have seen this people, and they are a stiff-necked people indeed! Let me alone, so that I may destroy them and blot out their name from under heaven. And I will make you into a nation stronger and more numerous than they.'

So I turned and went down from the mountain while it was ablaze with fire. And the two tablets of the covenant were in my hands. When I looked, I saw that you had sinned against the Lord your God; you had made for yourselves an idol cast in the shape of a calf. You had turned aside quickly from the way the Lord had commanded you. So I took the two tablets and threw them out of my hands, breaking them to pieces before your eyes.

Then once again I fell postrate before the Lord for forty days and forty nights; I ate no bread and drank no water, because of all the sin you had committed, doing what was evil in the Lord's sight and so provoking him to anger. I feared the anger and wrath of the Lord, for he was angry enough with you to destroy you......"

I lay postrate before the Lord those forty days and forty nights because the Lord said he would destroy you. I prayed to the Lord and said, "O Sovereign Lord, do not destroy your people, your own inheritance that you redeemed by your great power and brought out of Egypt with a mighty hand. Remember your servants Abraham, Isaac and Jacob. Overlook the stubbornness of this people, their wickedness and their sin. Otherwise, the country from which you brought us will say, 'Because the Lord was not able to take them into the land he had promised them, and because he hated them, he brought them out to put them to death in the desert.' But they are your people, your inheritance that you brought out by your great power and your outstretched arm."

> At that time the Lord said to me, "Chisel out two stone tablets like the first ones and come up to me on the mountain. Also make a wooden chest. I will write on the tablets the words that were on the first tablets, which you broke. Then you are to put them in the chest……"
> <u>Now I had stayed on the mountain forty days and nights, as I did the first time</u>, and the Lord listened to me at this time also. It was not his will to destroy you» (Deuteronomy 9:9-10:10).

The first 40 days and 40 nights that Moses spent on the mountain with God were done at God's invitation. Moses was shown the heavenly model of the tabernacle that he had to build and given the two tablets of stone that contained the covenant that the Lord had made with Israel.

The second 40 days and 40 nights that Moses spent on the mountain with God were different. Moses invited himself into God's presence. Things were very bad. The children of Israel had committed a dreadful sin and God wanted to destroy them. Moses said, "I fell postrate before the Lord for forty days and forty nights; I ate no bread and drank no water, because of all the sin you had committed, doing what was evil in the Lord's sight and so provoking him to anger. I feared the anger and wrath of the Lord, for he was angry enough with you to destroy you."

Moses was interceding. He was an intercessor. He was not just a prayer warrior. Norman Grubb wrote the following:

"A prayer warrior can pray for a thing to be done without necessarily being willing for the answer to come through himself; and he is not even bound to continue in the prayer until it is answered. But an intercessor is responsible to gain his objective, and he can never be free till he has gained it. He will go to any length for the prayer to be answered through himself."

Moses was an intercessor indeed. He was not carrying out a monologue with God. He was carrying out a dialogue with God. Let us look at two examples.

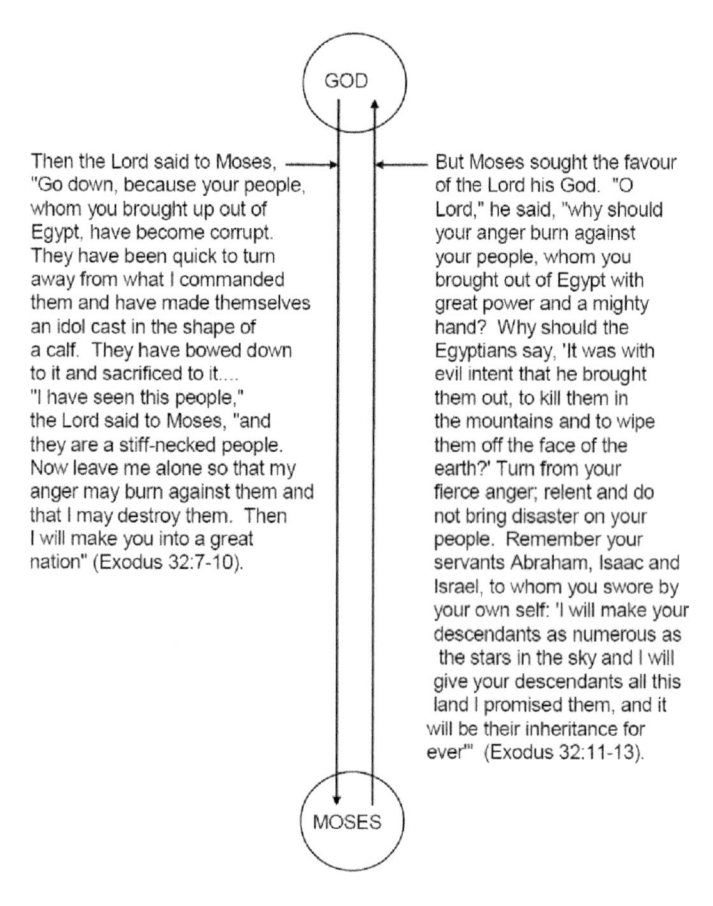

Then the Lord said to Moses, "Go down, because your people, whom you brought up out of Egypt, have become corrupt. They have been quick to turn away from what I commanded them and have made themselves an idol cast in the shape of a calf. They have bowed down to it and sacrificed to it.... "I have seen this people," the Lord said to Moses, "and they are a stiff-necked people. Now leave me alone so that my anger may burn against them and that I may destroy them. Then I will make you into a great nation" (Exodus 32:7-10).

But Moses sought the favour of the Lord his God. "O Lord," he said, "why should your anger burn against your people, whom you brought out of Egypt with great power and a mighty hand? Why should the Egyptians say, 'It was with evil intent that he brought them out, to kill them in the mountains and to wipe them off the face of the earth?' Turn from your fierce anger; relent and do not bring disaster on your people. Remember your servants Abraham, Isaac and Israel, to whom you swore by your own self: 'I will make your descendants as numerous as the stars in the sky and I will give your descendants all this land I promised them, and it will be their inheritance for ever'" (Exodus 32:11-13).

Moses was successful. The Bible says, "Then the Lord relented and did not bring on his people the disaster he had

WAITING ON THE LORD IN PRAYER

threatened." Moses succeeded because he did not leave the Lord God alone.

However, this was only part of the victory. All was not over. Consequently, the battle went on.

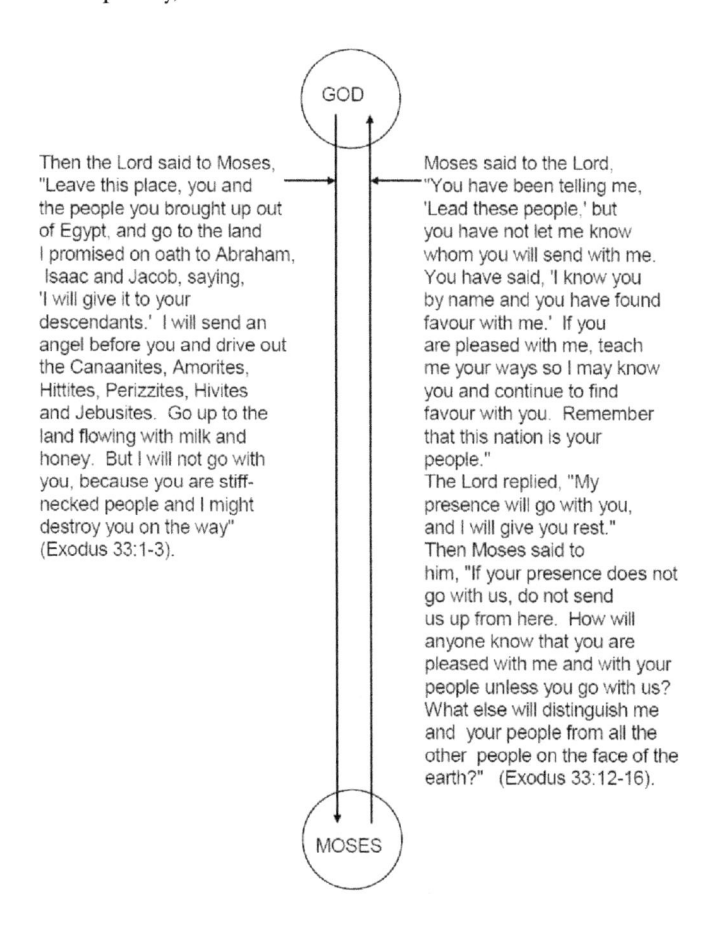

```
                    ┌─────┐
                    │ GOD │
                    └──┬──┘
                       │
Then the Lord said to Moses,     Moses said to the Lord,
"Leave this place, you and       "You have been telling me,
the people you brought up out    'Lead these people,' but
of Egypt, and go to the land     you have not let me know
I promised on oath to Abraham,   whom you will send with me.
Isaac and Jacob, saying,         You have said, 'I know you
'I will give it to your          by name and you have found
descendants.' I will send an     favour with me.' If you
angel before you and drive out   are pleased with me, teach
the Canaanites, Amorites,        me your ways so I may know
Hittites, Perizzites, Hivites    you and continue to find
and Jebusites. Go up to the      favour with you. Remember
land flowing with milk and       that this nation is your
honey. But I will not go with    people."
you, because you are stiff-      The Lord replied, "My
necked people and I might        presence will go with you,
destroy you on the way"          and I will give you rest."
(Exodus 33:1-3).                 Then Moses said to
                                 him, "If your presence does not
                                 go with us, do not send
                                 us up from here. How will
                                 anyone know that you are
                                 pleased with me and with your
                                 people unless you go with us?
                                 What else will distinguish me
                                 and your people from all the
                                 other people on the face of the
                                 earth?" (Exodus 33:12-16).
                    ┌───────┐
                    │ MOSES │
                    └───────┘
```

Again Moses was successful. The Bible says,

> "And the Lord said to Moses, "I will do the very thing

you have asked, because I am pleased with you and I know you by name" (Exodus 33:17).

THE CRITICAL NEED OF WAITING ON GOD IN PRAYER

What would have happened if when Israel sinned Moses knew nothing about waiting on God in prayer? The people would have reaped the full consequences of their sin. God would have destroyed them as He threatened. They would have been destroyed because their leader had no knowledge of the Spiritual Science of Waiting On God In Prayer.

As we have seen, the battle of intercession was very fierce. Moses laid postrate before God in battle for forty days and forty nights before he could succeed in moving God. Have you imagined what would have happened if Moses had been the kind of person who was given to indulgence and superficiality, so that he could only intercede for

1. one hour,
2. three hours,
3. six hours,
4. twelve hours or
5. twenty-four hours?

If that had been the limit of how far he could go, the nation would have perished. Even if he had developed muscles for spending

- three days,
- seven days,
- fourteen days,
- twenty-one days or
- twenty-eight days

before God, the nation would still have perished. It required the full 40 days and 40 nights of wrestling with God for him to win. God was not joking, and he did not stay longer than was necessary to have the Lord forgive the people and restore them!

What would have happened if by the time Israel sinned and desperately needed intercession, Moses himself had fallen into sin or was having a controversy with God? Again, the nation would have perished because he would not have been able to step at once into the office of intercession.

The future of someone,

1. a family,
2. an assembly,
3. a city,
4. a nation,
5. a continent,
6. a group of continents,
7. a work,
8. etc,

may depend on your capacity to wait before God in prayer some day. The best thing is for you to begin to prepare for that day, so that when it comes, you will be able to save the situation. This demands that you should establish a programme of learning to wait on God in prayer. We suggest that you should enroll in a personal School of Waiting On God In Prayer. There are a number of things to be learnt. First of all, there is the discipline of being separated from all human beings and being locked up in the presence of God. Secondly, there is the cultivation of a relationship with God that can permit you and Him to stay in each other's company for long. Thirdly, there is the cultivation of the art of talking to Him. Fourthly, there is the development of the art of hearing Him when He speaks. Lastly, there is the development of the art of wrestling with God until something that is His will is released by Him.

We suggest that since it is a matter of a relationship, and relationships have to be built and established, you plan a programme that could look like the following or one entirely of your own creation. We, however, insist that after you have established it, you follow it faithfully and rigorously in order to build the needed relationship with God:

- *Year 01: One hour of Waiting on God in Prayer*
- *Year 02: Three hours*
- *Year 03: Six hours*
- *Year 04: Twelve hours*
- *Year 05: Twenty-four hours*
- *Year 06: Thirty-six hours*
- *Year 07: Forty-eight hours*
- *Year 08: Seventy-two hours*
- *Year 09: 5 days*
- *Year 10: 7 days*
- *Year 11: 10 days*
- *Year 12: 14 days*
- *Year 13: 21 days*
- *Year 14: 28 days*
- *Year 15: 35 days*
- *Year 16: 40 days.*

We do hope that as you move on progressively, you will learn how to wait; how to know God, how to hunger for Him, how to hear His voice and how to wrestle with Him. It will be useless to lock yourself up for seven days and be totally bored and yearning for the days to be over! The goal of a programme like the above is to allow you to build a relationship with God that will make you feel that you needed more time with Him when your time of waiting on Him is over. It is also such that the joys of the previous seasons of waiting on Him will encourage you to press on, should He remain silent for long at the beginning of your time of waiting on Him in prayer.

DETERMINATION

It is important that all who want to deal with God should decide that they want to deal with Him. It is important that anyone who brings a problem to God should decide that the matter is of such importance that he will pursue it through, regardless of how difficult the pathway may be. It is also important that all who would deal with God decide that they will find their solution in God and find their solution nowhere else. Those who have alternatives to God should not bother to come to Him. He will be of no help to them.

Those who come to God with their problem knowing that they can be helped nowhere else are prepared to wait on God until He answers, regardless of how long it may take.

So Moses was lying postrate before God interceding increasingly. There was dialogue between the Lord God and himself.

Day 01 - He battled for 24 hours and received a 'No!'
Day 02 - He battled for 24 hours and received a 'No!'
Day 03 - He received a 'No!'
Day 05 - He received a 'No!'
Day 10 - He received a 'No!'
Day 20 - He received a 'No!'
Day 25 - He received a 'No!'
Day 30 - He received a 'No!'

Day 31 - He received a 'No!'
Day 32 - He received a 'No!'
Day 33 - He received a 'No!'
Day 34 - He received a 'No!'
Day 35 - He received a 'No!'
Day 36 - He received a 'No!'
Day 37 - He received a 'No!'
Day 38 - He received a 'No!'
Day 39 - He received a 'No!'
Day 40 - He received a 'Yes!'

Moses pressed on to the end. He had a problem that he could not lay aside. He also had a problem that only God could solve. So he clung to God until God solved the problem. He waited on God until the answer came from Him.

We shall see later on that it was good for Moses that the answer from the Lord did not come immediately. God never takes advantage of the sons of men. All that He does is for our good.

If He causes us to wait, it is for our good.

If He allows us to suffer, it is for our good.

If he allows us to be persecuted, it is for our good.

The Bible says,

> "And we know that in all things God works for the good of those who love him, who have been called according to his purpose"(Romans 8:28).

WAITING ON THE LORD IN PRAYER: THE EXAMPLE OF MOSES ON THE MOUNTAIN - 3

Then Moses said,

"Now show me your glory"(Exodus 33:18).

And the Lord said,

> "I will cause all my goodness to pass in front of you, and I will proclaim my name, the Lord, in your presence. I will have mercy on whom I will have mercy, and I will have compassion on whom I will have compassion. «But,» he said, "you cannot see my face, for no-one may see me and live."
> Then the Lord said, "There is a place near me where you may stand on a rock. When my glory passes by, I will put you in a cleft in the rock and cover you with my hand until I have passed by. Then I will remove my hand and you will see my back; but my face must not be seen."
> The Lord said to Moses, "Chisel out two stone tablets like the first ones, and I will write on them the

words that were on the first tablets, which you broke. Be ready in the morning, and then come up on Mount Sinai. Present yourself to me there on top of the mountain. No one is to come with you or be seen anywhere on the mountain; not even the flocks and herds may graze in front of the mountain."

So Moses chiseled out two stone tablets like the first ones and went up Mount Sinai early in the morning, as the Lord had commanded him; and he carried the two stone tablets in his hands. Then the Lord came down in the cloud and stood there with him and proclaimed his name, the Lord. And he passed in front of Moses, proclaiming, "The Lord, the Lord, the compassionate and gracious God, slow to anger, abounding in love and faithfulness, maintaining love to thousands, and forgiving wickedness, rebellion and sin. Yet he does not leave the guilty unpunished; he punishes the children and their children for the sin of the fathers to the third and fourth generation"

Moses bowed to the ground at once and worshipped"(Exodus 33:18-34:8).

Moses wanted to behold the Lord!

He asked the Lord, "Now, show me your glory."

One thing that is generally absent in the spiritual experiences of many believers is that the Lord has never appeared to them. Yet the Bible is full of instances when God appeared to people. Let us look at a few of these:

1. *"When Abram was ninety-nine years old, the Lord appeared to him and said, 'I am God Almighty; walk before me and*

be blameless. I will confirm my covenant between me and you and will greatly increase your numbers" (Genesis 17:1-2).
2. *"The Lord appeared to Abraham near the great trees of Mamre while he was sitting on the entrance to his tent in the heat of the day"(Genesis 18:1).*
3. *"The Lord appeared to Isaac and said, 'Do not go down to Egypt; live in the land where I tell you to live'" (Genesis 26:2).*
4. *"That night the Lord appeared to him and said, 'I am the God of your father Abraham. Do not be afraid, for I am with you; I will bless you and will increase the number of your descendants for the sake of my servant Abraham'" (Genesis 26:24).*
5. *«After Jacob returned from Paddan Aram, God appeared to him again and blessed him»(Genesis 35:9).*
6. *«There the angel of the Lord appeared to him in flames of fire from within a bush»(Exodus 3:2).*
7. *«When the angel of the Lord appeared to Gideon, he said, 'The Lord is with you, mighty warrior'" (Judges 6:12).*
8. *"The angel of the Lord appeared to her and said, "You are sterile and childless, but you are going to conceive and have a son"(Judges 13:3).*
9. *«The Lord continued to appear at Shiloh, and there he revealed himself to Samuel through his word»(1 Samuel 3:21).*
10. *«Then an angel of the Lord appeared to him, standing at the right side of the altar of incense" (Luke 1:11).*

A.W. Tozer said,

> "For several generations the evangelical Christian world has run on hearsay. We look back pensively to the fathers who met God in brilliant and

satisfying encounter. We quote them lovingly and try to draw what spiritual nourishment we can from the knowledge that the High and Lofty One once manifested Himself to wondering men. We pour over the record of his self-revelations to men like Abraham, Jacob, Moses and Isaiah. We read with longing hearts how once 'the place was shaken where they were assembled together; and they were all filled with the Holy Spirit, and they spake the word of God with boldness» (Acts 4:31).

We read the stories of Edwards and Finney, and our hearts yearn to see again a shining forth of the glory of God."

These people wanted to behold the glory of God. They sought God. They waited on God and the Lord revealed Himself to them.

Moses had known God for many years. The Lord had appeared to him in the form of an angel. The Lord had spoken to him many times. The Lord had performed outstanding miracles through his instrumentality. There was so much between him and God. However, Moses wanted more of God.

It has been said that hunger for God is directly proportional to the knowledge one has of Him.

>   No knowledge of God ---> No hunger for God.
> Little knowledge of God ---> Little hunger for God.
> Average knowledge of God ---> Average hunger for God.
> Great knowledge of God ---> Great hunger for God.

Knowledge of God (y-axis)

Hunger for God (x-axis)

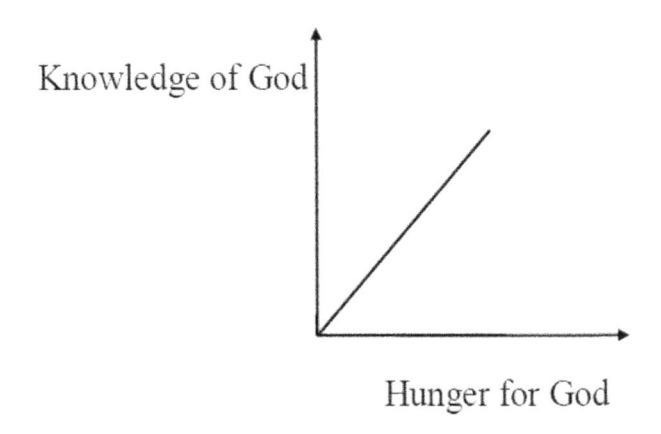

The Apostle Paul also had great encounters with God and great revelations from the Lord. These, however, only served to create a greater hunger for the Lord. He said,

"About noon as I came near Damascus, suddenly a bright light from heaven flashed around me. I fell to the ground and heard a voice say to me, "Saul! Saul! Why do you persecute me?' 'Who are you, Lord?' I asked. 'I am Jesus of Nazareth, whom you are persecuting,' he replied»(Acts 22:6-8).

"One night, the Lord spoke to Paul in a vision: 'Do not be afraid; keep on speaking, do not be silent. For I am with you, and no-one is going to attack and harm you, because I have many people in this city.' So Paul stayed for a year and a half, teaching them the word of God»(Acts 18:9-11).

"God did extraordinary miracles through Paul, so that even handkerchiefs and aprons that had touched him were taken to the sick, and their illnesses were cured and the evil spirits left them"(Acts 19:11-12).

"I must go on boasting. Although there is nothing to be gained, I will go on to visions and revelations from the Lord"(2 Corinthians 12:1).

Yes, many revelations, abundant manifestations of God's power, much fruitful labors. Should he seek anything again? Yes, he sought the Lord. He wanted Jesus. He wanted more and more of the Lord Jesus! His heart cry was for Jesus. He confessed,

"I want to know Christ" (Philippians 3:10).

He knew Christ, but he wanted to know more of Him.

He knew Christ much, but he wanted to know Him as he had never known Him. The knowledge that he had from the encounters, visions and revelations only set him aflame with hunger for the Lord Jesus!

NOW SHOW ME YOUR GLORY

Moses wanted to behold the glory of the Lord. He wanted to see the Lord Himself.

Was it ambition? No, it was spiritual hunger!

He did not say, "Lord, will You show me Your glory some day?" He wanted to behold God's glory immediately. He was hungry for God. Who, when he is hungry now, wants food for tomorrow instead of for now?

There are many who are satisfied because they know that they will see the Lord that Day! They are not lovers. Lovers want to see the Beloved now. If they cannot see Him in fullness now, they at least hunger for all that they can see of Him now. They will consequently wait on Him, so that He may reveal Himself in any form that He can reveal Himself now. It may not be the total picture, but it will go some distance to quench the thirst and to create more intense thirst! It is like someone who cannot see the one he loves, but who is shown a photograph of that one. The photograph will be precious. He will cherish it even though it will create hunger for the real person.

Moses knew he could not see God as he would see Him some day in glory, but he wanted to see all that God could allow him see of Him then.

> God consented!
> God consented!!
> God consented!!!

GOD SHOWED HIS GLORY TO MOSES

When we confront the fact that too many believers have never seen anything of the glory of the Lord with the fact that the Lord God Almighty wants to reveal His glory to His children, we are stupefied by the few who have seen Him!

Moses asked, "Now show me your glory," and the Lord answered, "I will cause all my goodness to pass in front of you, and I will proclaim My name, the Lord, in your presence.

Moses asked to be shown God's glory.

God decided to:

1. *Cause all His goodness to pass in front of Moses.*
2. *Proclaim His name, the Lord, in Moses' presence.*

The Lord was giving Moses more than what he (Moses) had asked. Indeed how true is the Scripture which says,

> "<u>Now to him who is able to do immeasurably more than all we ask or imagine</u>, according to his power that is at work within us, to him be glory in the church and in Christ Jesus throughout all generations, for ever and ever! Amen" (Ephesians 3:20-21).

The Lord is more anxious to reveal Himself to us than we are anxious to have Him reveal Himself to us!

God decided to cause all His goodness to pass in front of Moses and to proclaim His Name to Moses' hearing. He gave His word to Moses. Then the Lord confronted the fact that if He was to cause all His goodness to pass before Moses, he (Moses) would see His face and die. There was a problem, and had the Lord been unwilling to show Moses His glory, He would have said to Moses, "Let us drop the matter. It will cost you your life."

God was, however, anxious to reveal His glory to Moses, and so He decided to solve the problem! He said,

> "There is a place near me where you may stand on a rock. When my glory passes by, I will put you in a cleft in the rock and cover you with my hand until I have passed by. Then I will remove my hand and you will see my back; but my face you must not see" (Exodus 33:21-23).

God solved the problem!

God let all His goodness pass before Moses!

God proclaimed His Name before Moses.

God proclaimed His character - slow to anger, abounding in love, etc.

Moses bowed to the ground at once and worshipped!

The Lord Jesus taught,

> "So I say to you: Ask and it will be given to you; seek and you will find; knock and the door will be opened to you. For everyone who asks receives; he who seeks finds; and to him who knocks, the door will be opened" (Luke 11:9-10).

Have you ever asked the Lord to show you His glory?

Have you ever sought the Lord to show you His glory?

Have you ever knocked for the Lord to show you His glory?

> "You do not have, because you do not ask God"(James 4:2).

MOSES' BEHOLDING THE GLORY OF GOD (A PARENTHESIS)

You will remember that the request of Moses to the Lord for the glory of the Lord to be shown to him came during the fierce battle of intercession for the salvation of the people of Israel. That is why immediately the glory of the Lor

> d passed before him, he immediately continued to intercede, "O Lord, if I have found favour in your eyes," he said, "then let the Lord go with us. Although this is a stiff-necked people, forgive our

wickedness and our sin, and take us as your inheritance" (Exodus 34:9).

He yielded. He said,

> "I am making a covenant with you. Before all your people I will do wonders never before done in any nation in the world. The people you live among will see how awesome is the work that I, the Lord, will do for you" (Exodus 34:10).

So Moses invested forty days and forty nights lying postrate before God interceding for the children of Israel. It was a costly investment for others. In the course of it, he sought for God's glory and it was revealed to him in full abundance.

The one who invests in the Lord is no loser. God will fend for him. The one who invests in others is no loser. God will fend for him.

The Israelites were spared death and restored to God! Moses beheld the glory of the Lord!

Is that enough reward for forty days and forty nights of waiting on God in fasting and prayer?

We leave the answer with you!

Will you do the same for others?

Will you go away and fast and pray for

1. one week,
2. two weeks,
3. three weeks,
4. four weeks,
5. five weeks,

6. six weeks, etc,

that

- someone,
- some family,
- some quarter,
- some village, town or city,
- some nation,
- some continent or
- some continents

may come to the salvation or to the fullness of our God? If you do, you may be surprised by what will happen between God and you as a parenthesis or as a bonus! Amen.

WAITING ON THE LORD IN PRAYER: THE EXAMPLE OF MOSES ON THE MOUNTAIN - 4

"When Moses came down from Mount Sinai with the two tablets of the Testimony in his hands, he was not aware that his face was radiant because he had spoken with the Lord. When Aaron and all the Israelites saw Moses, his face was radiant, and they were afraid to come near him. But Moses called to them, so Aaron and all the leaders of the community came back to him, and he spoke to them. Afterwards all the Israelites came near him, and he gave them all the commands the Lord gave him on Mount Sinai.

When Moses finished speaking to them, he put a veil over his face. But whenever he entered the Lord's presence to speak with him, he removed the veil until he came out. And when he came out and told the Israelites what he had been commanded, they saw that his face was radiant. Then Moses would put the veil back on his face until he went in to speak with the Lord" (Exodus 34:29-35).

Moses was on the mountain for forty days in the immediate presence of God. He was caught up with wrestling in intercession for the Israelites. He was in the immediate environment of God, and as he stayed in the presence of God, some of the glory of God was being transferred to him. The consequence of that transfer of glory was that his face became radiant. He had put on the radiance of God. He had put on God. He had put on God unconsciously. The glory of God just flowed to him without his knowing it, a little at a time from the time he first entered into His presence, until the time he left His presence.

If Moses had been in God's presence for a short time, there would have been very little glory of God transferred to him for it to be noticeable. However, after forty days, what could not be seen after a few days was manifest.

God gives Himself away to those who wait before Him. He leaves His marks on those who wait before Him.

> No waiting on God ---> No marks of God in that life.
> Little waiting on God ---> Little marks of God on that life.
> Average waiting on God ---> Some marks of God on that life.
> Long waiting on God ---> Many marks of God on that life.
> Sustained waiting on God ---> Sustained marks of God on that life.
> Permanent waiting on God ---> Permanent marks of God on that life.

How much of God one puts on is directly proportional to how much time has been spent in the presence of God. We can present this fact as follows:

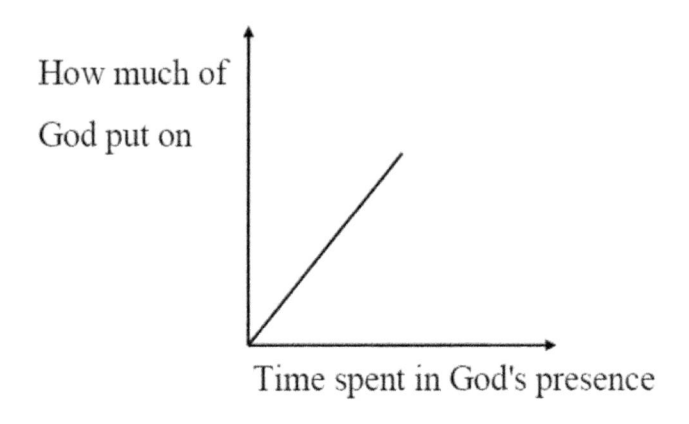

How much of God put on (y-axis) vs *Time spent in God's presence* (x-axis) — a straight line with positive slope.

Two believers can believe on the same day, and years afterwards they are so different. One bears the marks of God and the other does not. What caused the difference? The difference came from the fact that one waited on the Lord and the other did not. One frequented the presence of the Lord and the other did not. One dwelt in the presence of the Lord and the other did not. One hungered after God and did something about that hunger, and the other did not. One sought the presence of God and the other did not.

Moses confessed,

> "Lord, you have been our dwelling place throughout all generations" (Psalm 90:1),

and he certainly knew what he was proclaiming.

The Psalmist proclaimed,

> "He who dwells in the shelter of the Most High will rest in the shadow of the Almighty" (Psalm 91:1). He continued, "If you make the Most High your dwelling - even the Lord, who is my refuge - then no harm will befall you, no disaster will come near your tent" (Psalm 91:9-10).

The Lord Jesus laboured to dwell in the presence of God. We can say that He lived in the presence of His Father and withdrew from time to time to meet the needs of men, and this was the work His Father wanted Him to do. Is it surprising that He was full of the Holy Spirit from Bethlehem to the Cross?

How much of God a person puts on also depends on the intensity of his pursuit of God during the time spent waiting before the Lord. Say two people withdrew to wait on God for one week. One gave himself exclusively to seeking the Lord, opening his heart to the Lord, confessing all his sins to the Lord and forsaking them whole-heartedly, and then crying out to the Lord night and day with fasting. The other confessed lightly and superficially, forsook sin partially, and was set on light-hearted restitution. He slept most of the time and concentrated on reading the Bible and some other books and not on seeking the Lord and waiting on Him. After the seven days both would return to people, but what they would have put on of God would be vastly different.

How much one puts on of the Lord during a certain amount of time of waiting on Him is directly proportional to the intensity of waiting on Him.

Little Intensity of Waiting on Him ---> Little Marks of God put on

Average Intensity of Waiting on Him ---> Some Marks of God put on

Great Intensity of Waiting on Him ---> Deep Marks of God put on

We can also present this as follows:

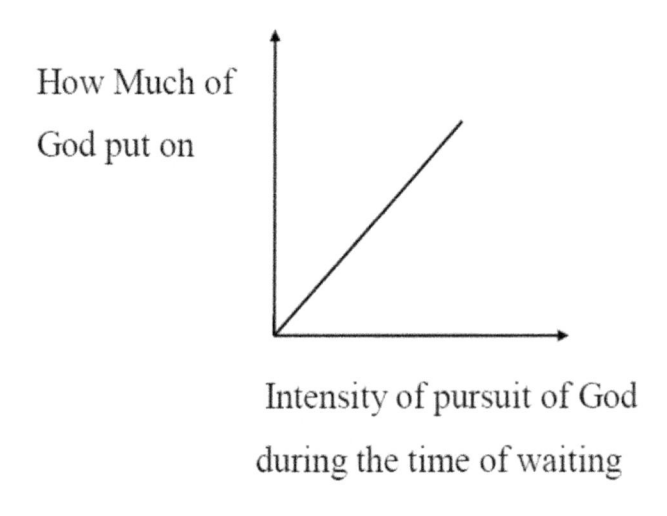

How Much of God put on (y-axis)

Intensity of pursuit of God during the time of waiting (x-axis)

Moses obviously sought God with his whole might during the forty days and forty nights that were spent in God's presence. The long duration and the great intensity combined to produce the radiance that caused Moses and the leaders to hesitate to draw near to him.

WHERE IS THE RADIANCE?

People could begin to withdraw for three days,

1. five days,
2. seven days,

3. ten days,
4. fourteen days,
5. twenty-one days,
6. etc,

and lock themselves somewhere to seek the Lord, to wait on God in prayer. This will be an encouraging sign in the horizon, and we eagerly wait for that sign to appear. It will be indicative of the soon-coming of great things.

However, if you withdraw and wait before the Lord, do wait upon Him indeed. Wait for Him long enough and with deepest intensity, so that when you come back from your seven, ten or fourteen days with Him, people will not need to be told that you went away to wait on God. The radiance will tell the story.

In all waiting on God that results in an encounter between the Living God and the waiting believer, there are marks that ought to last a lifetime or so. These marks ought to speak for themselves.

Isaiah encountered the Lord. The Bible reports:

> «In the year that King Uzziah died, I saw the Lord seated on a throne, high and exalted, and the train of his robe filled the temple. Above him were seraphs, each with six wings: with two wings they covered their faces, with two they covered their feet, and with two they were flying. And they were calling to one another:
> "Holy, holy, holy is the Lord Almighty,
> the whole earth is full of his glory."
> At the sound of their voices the doorposts and

thresholds shook and the temple was filled with smoke.

"Woe to me!" I cried. "I am ruined! For I am a man of unclean lips, and I live among a people of unclean lips, and my eyes have seen the King, the Lord Almighty."

Then one of the seraphs flew to me with a live coal in his hand, which he had taken with tongs from the altar. With it he touched my mouth and said, "See, this has touched your lips; your guilt is taken away and your sin atoned for."

Then I heard the voice of the Lord saying, "Whom shall I send? And who will go for us?"

And I said, "Here am I. Send me!"

He said, 'Go and tell this people:

"Be ever hearing, but never understanding;

be ever seeing, but never perceiving"'(Isaiah 6:1-9).

When Isaiah encountered the Lord, he heard the seraphs talk. What were they pre-occupied with? They were proclaiming, "Holy, holy, holy is the Lord Almighty, the whole earth is full of his glory." They were pre-occupied with the holiness of God as priority number one and the glory of the Lord as priority number two. When Moses first encountered the Lord, he was told,

> "Take off your sandals, for the place where you are standing is holy ground" (Exodus 3:5).

When Joshua encountered the Lord he was told,

> "Take off your sandals, for the place where you are standing is holy"(Joshua 5:15).

The music of heaven is "Holy, holy, holy is the Lord God Almighty, who was, and is, and is to come"(Revelation 4:8).

Brooks says,

"A person of real holiness is much affected and taken up in the admiration of the holiness of God. Unholy persons may be somewhat affected and taken with the other excellencies of God; it is only holy souls that are taken and affected with His holiness."

The angels are caught up with His holiness. God seeks holiness as priority number one in His elect. The immature are preoccupied with doing things for God. The mature are taken up with God's holiness.

The first time when the Lord appeared to me, His holiness was such that all I could do was to crawl under the bed and hide, totally unable to look at Him any further. The first time, when I spent forty nights consecutively, praying the whole night alone, the Lord invested the first nine nights in exposing the rottenness and corruption of my heart and leading me to repentance and restitution. It was on the tenth night that I could then pray for others.

God first dealt with Isaiah's sin before He could commission him.

It is most likely that if you wait before the Lord long enough for Him to decide to do serious business with you, the first thing He will like to show you is His holiness and your sin. He will like to deal with your sin, so that He might commission you!

It should be clearly understood that until God has worked out His holiness in a person, the person is of little use to Him.

Isaiah encountered God. Two marks were left to prove this - his cleansing and his commissioning.

If you too really wait on God, you will come from the waiting with marks. If the marks are lacking, it will be proof that the Lord was not encountered.

> "And we who with unveiled faces all contemplate the Lord's glory, are being transformed into his likeness with ever-increasing glory, which comes from the Lord, who is the Spirit" (2 Corinthians 4:18).

12

WAITING ON THE LORD IN PRAYER: THE EXAMPLE OF THE 120 DISCIPLES

"Then opened he their understanding, that they might understand the scriptures. And he said unto them, Thus it is written, and thus it behoved Christ to suffer, and to rise from the dead the third day: And that repentance and remission of sins should be preached in his name among all nations, beginning at Jerusalem. And we are witnesses of these things. And, behold, I send the promise of my Father upon you: but tarry ye in the city of Jerusalem, until ye be endued with power from on high.

And he led them out as far as to Bethany, and he lifted up his hands, and blessed them. And it came to pass, while he blessed them, he was parted from them, and carried up into heaven.

And they worshipped him, and returned to Jerusalem with great joy: And were continually in the temple, praising and blessing God. Amen." (Luke 24:45-53, KJV).

"In my former book, Theophilus, I wrote about all

that Jesus began to do and to teach until the day he was taken up to heaven, after giving instructions through the Holy Spirit to the apostles he had chosen. After his suffering, he showed himself to these men and gave many convincing proofs that he was alive. He appeared to them over a period of forty days and spoke about the kingdom of God. On one occasion, while he was eating with them, he gave them this command: 'Do not leave Jerusalem , but wait for the gift my Father promised, which you have heard me speak about. For John baptized with water, but in a few days you will be baptized with the Holy Spirit.'

So when they met together, they asked him, 'Lord, are you at this time going to restore the kingdom to Israel?'

He said to them: 'It is not for you to know the times or dates the Father has set by his own authority. But you will receive power when the Holy Spirit comes on you; and you will be my witnesses in Jerusalem, and in all Judea and Samaria, and to the ends of the earth.'

After he said this, he was taken up before their very eyes, and a cloud hid him from their sight……

Then they returned to Jerusalem from the hill called the Mount of Olives, a Sabbath day's walk from the city. When they arrived, they went upstairs to the room where they were staying. Those present were Peter, John, James and Andrew; Philip and Thomas, Bartholomew and Matthew; James the son of Alphaeus and Simon the Zealot, and Judas son of James. They all joined together constantly in prayer, along with the women and Mary the mother of Jesus, and with his brothers……

> When the day of Pentecost came, they were all together in one place. Suddenly a sound like the blowing of a violent wind came from heaven and filled the whole house where they were sitting. They saw what seemed to be tongues of fire that separated and came to rest on each of them. All of them were filled with the Holy Spirit and began to speak in other tongues as the Spirit enabled them" (Acts 1:1-2:4).

The 120 brethren who gathered in the Upper Room were all disciples of the Lord Jesus and some of them were the apostles. They were saved and some of them had performed extraordinary miracles. After the resurrection, the Lord Jesus revealed Himself to them. They were with Him at the Mountain of Olives where they worshipped Him and received His blessings. They then returned to Jerusalem with great joy.

What if they had just gone away, each one to his own house and then each tried single-handedly to win the world for Him? It would have been a great failure. What if, after that, they had banded themselves together and tried to win Jerusalem and the rest of the world for Him? It would have been a great disaster!

They had to tarry in Jerusalem until they were endued with power from on high.

They waited on the Lord in prayer. They did not know when the Holy Spirit would come. So they were alert. They were waiting night and day. They were in prayer night and day.

They suspended sleep.
They suspended chatting.

They suspended eating.

They were desperate to have the promised power, and so no price was too great to be paid. Those who normally slept much abandoned sleep. Those who were normally given to food forwent food. They wanted something that was greater than food. They wanted something big, and so they were prepared to pay a big price. The value of a thing is directly proportional to the price paid for it.

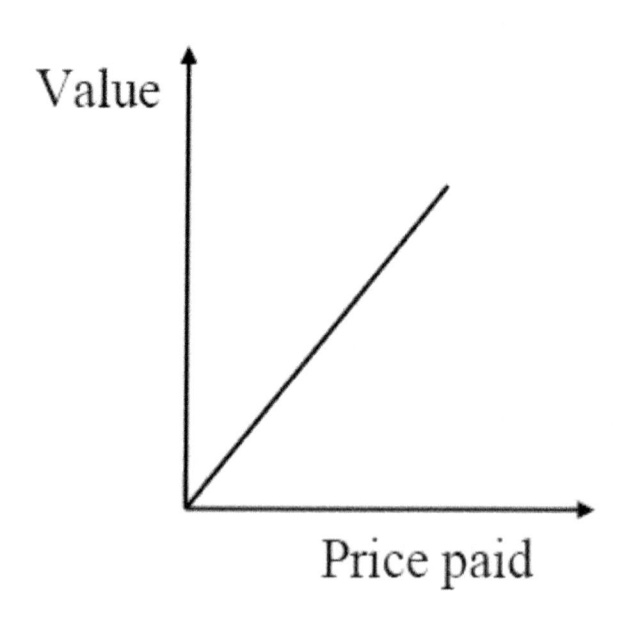

Could that be the problem with your spiritual life? You have perhaps preferred to pay no price, content to receive that which God gives to all. Do you realize that you have perhaps robbed yourself of God's best? It can be clearly said that after salvation which is a free gift, much in the Christian life depends on the price paid.

No price paid ---> Nothing received.
Little price paid ---> Little received.
Much price paid ---> Much received.
Extreme price paid ---> Extreme abundance received.

- The 120 waited on God in prayer for the
- first day and nothing happened;
- second day and nothing happened;
- third day and nothing happened;
- fourth day and nothing happened;
- fifth day and nothing happened;
- sixth day and nothing happened;
- seventh day and nothing happened;
- eighth day and nothing happened; and
- ninth day and nothing happened.

If they had grown weary and tired and gone away on the ninth day, they would just have been like those who had not waited at all! There are many believers who start on some course with the Lord, make some progress, but give up before the Lord's blessings come. May the Lord help you not to be like them!

The Bible exhorts,

> "You sympathized with those in prison and joyfully accepted the confiscating of your property, because you knew that you yourselves had better and lasting possessions. So do not throw away your confidence; it will be richly rewarded." <u>You need to persevere so that when you have done the will of God, you receive what he has promised</u>. For in just a very little while, 'he who is coming will come and will not delay. <u>But my righteous one will live by</u>

> faith. And if he shrinks back, I will not be pleased with him.' But we are not of those who shrink back and are destroyed, but of those who believe and are saved"(Hebrews 10:34-39).

The 120 waited on God in prayer for the tenth day and the Holy Spirit came down upon them, and the world has never been the same since He came down on that day!!

WILL YOU TOO WAIT ON GOD IN PRAYER FOR TEN DAYS?

I want to suggest to you that you should withdraw somewhere and give yourself to ten days of waiting on God in prayer. Fast for those ten days of waiting and see what will happen between you and God.

I want to suggest that the elders of your church should withdraw and lock themselves somewhere for ten days of waiting on God in prayer with fasting, and see what will happen to them, to the church they lead and to the lost in the city in which they are elders. Amen.

13

WAITING ON THE LORD IN PRAYER: THE EXAMPLE OF ERLO STEGEN

It was the year 1966. For twelve years Erlo had only preached repentance. Many times during this period, the tent was taken down, only to be pitched again in another place in Zululand. Thousands of messages were given and tens of thousands came to listen -- inquisitive, scared, but also noisy. Many activities were undertaken, self-sacrificial work, but what was achieved through this? The answer to this question made Erlo deeply unhappy. Did he not say that he did not want to play church? Where then was the fruit of his work? In the early church there was power, conversions and true life and that is what he desired. All that he could see was a form of godliness.

God had already done something. He had brought Erlo to this dead end. He had shown him his spiritual poverty. He had extinguished the fire of human zeal so that He could kindle His heavenly fire.

Erlo Stegen called a few members of the community together and confessed his reluctance to continue on the same road. Together they began to seek an answer. They would come together twice a day and study the Book of Acts. In a small corrugated iron building which had been a stable, they met to pray and study the Bible.

Erlo was acutely aware of the danger of biblism and did not want to study only those verses which they liked. "We did not want to be like children who look for all the raisins in a cake." He took John 7:38 as their point of departure: "Whoever believes in Me, as the Scripture has said, streams of living water will flow from within him." He asked those who were present if they believed? After they had all answered affirmatively, he asked out of whose life the living water flowed. Not one of them could testify of living water. He came to the conclusion: either they were not speaking the truth, or their faith was not right, or the Bible was wrong. They had prayed that God would work among the heathens, but it became clear to them that God did not want to begin with the heathens, but with them. They looked at their own lives and realized how sinful they were. From the story of Ananias and Sapphira, they saw that it was better that they should die, than that sin should be brought into the community." The further we got, the more our hearts broke." They began to see themselves more clearly in the light of the Word and through the conviction of the Holy Spirit. God did not have the first place in their lives. This is one of the conditions for revival.

They also read in John 16:18 that the Holy Spirit came to convict the world of sin and righteousness and judgment. This is what is experienced in a mighty way in a revival.

One Saturday, the evening Bible Study was shifted to the afternoon. The place where they were gathered was an old stable next to the tennis courts where the magistrate and well known whites of the village were playing tennis. Erlo wanted to close the windows so that the tennis players would not hear that he was praying together with black people. He could not send the blacks home. While he was closing the windows it was as if a voice said to him: "Close the windows - but then I too will remain outside. I will not come in. You are ashamed of Me."

"It was true! I had been ashamed of Him and suddenly it did not matter who heard me cry.... I did cry." Like Peter of old he cried. He realized that he himself was the greatest stumbling block in the way of revival. His problem was pride and the Bible says: "God resists the proud." He realized that not only the devil but even God was against him.

Another important point on which he was convicted was his lack of love for the black man. He realized that God could not use him unless he changed in this area. "My relationship to the least is my relationship to Christ. As close as I am to that man, nothing closer am I to Christ." In the meanwhile, the Lord was also working with the congregation and the morning after he had got rid of his judgment against the blacks, they called him "Baba" (Father) for the first time; a name which they never used for a white man.

In this way, the Lord broke down one barrier after another, so preparing the way for the victory of the Spirit. The burden of sin in his life became so heavy for him that he came to the point where he forgot that he was ever a child of the Lord. All that stood before him was his sin. The only thing that he could pray at that moment was: "God have mercy upon me, I am a sinner." His sin stood in the way of the blessing of the Lord.

While they were busy with the story of Peter and John and the cripple who was healed outside the temple (Acts 3), they noticed that Peter said: "Look at us." They asked themselves whether they could tell the people to look at them, at their life style and their relationship with the Lord. He also noted that Peter and John had no money. He then told the story of two priests who counted the money after a service. The older priest said to the younger priest: "Peter can no longer say, 'Silver and gold have I not.'" The young priest answered: "Yes, but he can also no longer say, 'In the Name of Jesus Christ the Nazarene, stand up and walk'." That which the first church had (power) they did not have, but that which the first church did not have (money), that they had. After he had told this, a young girl who had come to repentance only three months before stood up and asked if she could pray. "I can no longer endure this situation of powerlessness," she said while tears streamed down her cheeks. Erlo gave permission and she prayed: "Lord, won't You allow your fire to burn in our hearts, that we will truly live as the Bible commands?"

Erlo was so touched by this prayer that he immediately closed the service. After the meeting he said to his brother, Friedel: "If this prayer was of the Holy Spirit, and I believe it was, then the God of old will once again be in our midst." Erlo had longed many times for this heavenly fire. He knew that only a spiritual awakening, a revival worked through the Holy Spirit, could breathe life into his own dead bones and those of his fellow believers and all the heathens. He reminded himself of Kurt Koch's prayer in 1963. He prayed for revival in Zululand after he had spoken of the reality of the Holy Spirit at the Lutheran Theological Seminary at Mapumulo. While the girl prayed, it was for Erlo as if his heart was warming like that of the men on the road to Emmaus, when Jesus Christ Himself walked and spoke with them.

"And then after about a week, God came down." Suddenly there was a mighty wind, almost like compressed air which is released. It felt like a wind which blew through them. The building shook and everyone was aware that God was in their midst. Erlo Shegen buried his face in his hands, deeply aware of his unworthiness. He felt that he should bow down low. Everybody was on their knees. No one could grasp it. Revival had begun. The Spirit had filled the small group in the old stable where they had gathered. From that moment onwards, everything was different.

— WELLY DU TOIT, "GOD'S GRACE." THE REVIVAL AT KWA SIZABANTU, PAGES 29-31

WHAT IF THEY HAD NOT WAITED ON GOD?

What if they had not waited on God in prayer and the study of the Word?

Are you where they were? Have you continued in human energy, human zeal, human arrangements, etc., for days, weeks, months and years?

Is your entire work the fruit of man's work? Where are the marks of the Holy Spirit's presence and work?

If you are where they were, won't you do what they did - put aside the labors of the flesh in the power of the flesh and turn radically and totally to the Lord, and wait on Him in prayer until He acts?

Won't you do that today?

Won't you do that now?

14

WAITING ON THE LORD IN PRAYER: THE EXAMPLE OF SAUL OF TARSUS - 1

«Meanwhile, Saul was still breathing out murderous threats against the Lord's disciples. He went to the high priest and asked him for letters to the synagogues in Damascus, so that if he found any there who belonged to the Way, whether men or women, he might take them as prisoners to Jerusalem. As he neared Damascus on his journey, suddenly a light from heaven flashed around him. He fell to the ground and heard a voice say to him, "Saul, Saul, why do you persecute me?"

"Who are you, Lord?" Saul asked. "I am Jesus, whom you are persecuting," he replied. "Now get up and go into the city, and you will be told what you must do."

The men traveling with Saul stood there speechless; they heard the sound but did not see anyone. Saul got up from the ground, but when he opened his eyes he could see nothing. So they led him by the hand into Damascus. For three days he was blind and did not eat or drink anything.

> In Damascus there was a disciple named Ananias. The Lord called him in a vision, "Ananias!" "Yes, Lord," he answered. The Lord told him, "Go to the house of Judas on Straight Street and ask for a man from Tarsus named Saul, for he is praying. In a vision he has seen a man named Ananias come and place his hands on him to restore him to sight."
>
> "Lord," Ananias answered, "I have heard many reports about this man and all the harm he has done to your saints in Jerusalem. And he has come here with authority from the chief priests to arrest all who call on your name."
>
> But the Lord said to Ananias, "Go! This man is my chosen instrument to carry my name before the Gentiles and their kings and before the people of Israel. I will show him how much he must suffer for my name."
>
> Then Ananias went to the house and entered it. Placing his hands on Saul, he said, "Brother Saul, the Lord -Jesus, who appeared to you on the road as you were coming here - has sent me so that you may see again and be filled with the Holy Spirit." Immediately, something like scales fell from Saul's eyes, and he could see again. He got up and was baptized, and after taking some food, he regained his strength"(Acts 9:1-19).

From the very beginning of his encounter and walk with God, Saul of Tarsus had dialogues with the Lord. For example:

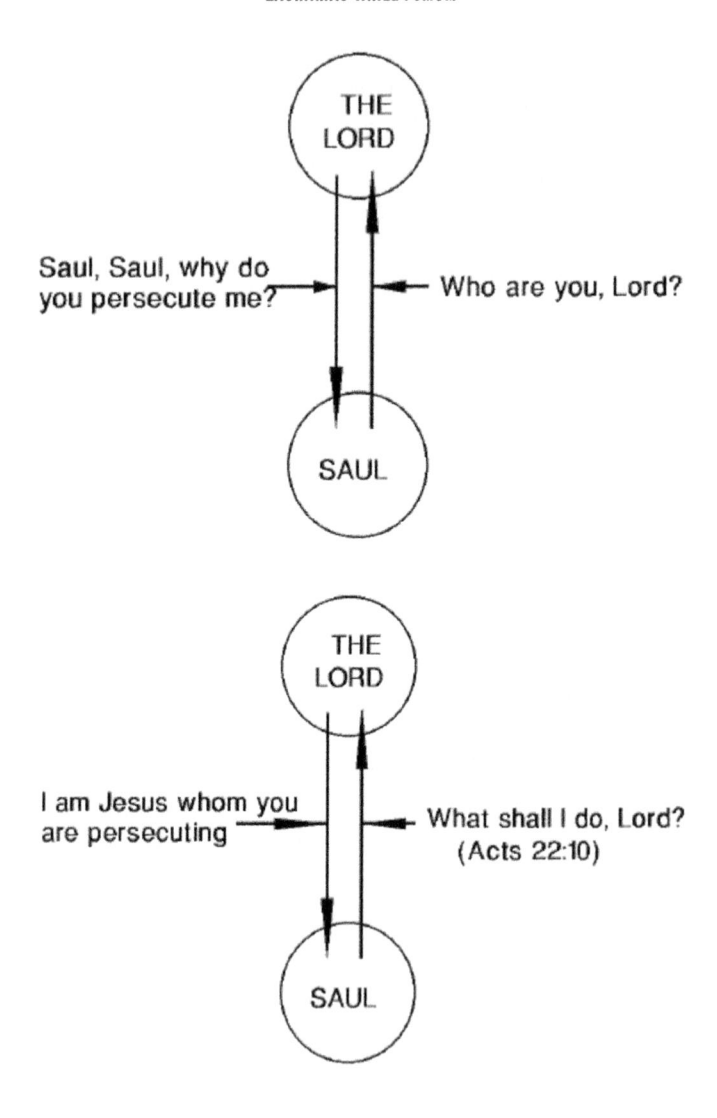

```
         THE
         LORD
           ↕
Saul, Saul, why do          Who are you, Lord?
you persecute me? →       ←
           ↕
         SAUL
```

```
         THE
         LORD
           ↕
I am Jesus whom you         What shall I do, Lord?
are persecuting  →        ←    (Acts 22:10)
           ↕
         SAUL
```

How impossible it would have been for Saul to make progress if the Lord had spoken all the time! How impossible it would have been for Saul to make progress if he had spoken all the time!

What if Saul had heard the Lord say, "Saul, Saul, why do you persecute me?" and had not asked, "Who are you, Lord?" It would have been impossible for the Lord to reveal Himself further to him.

What if Saul had asked, "Who are you, Lord?" and received no answer? Would he have been able to go on and ask, "What shall I do, Lord?"

Even in talking to Ananias, God and he had a dialogue:

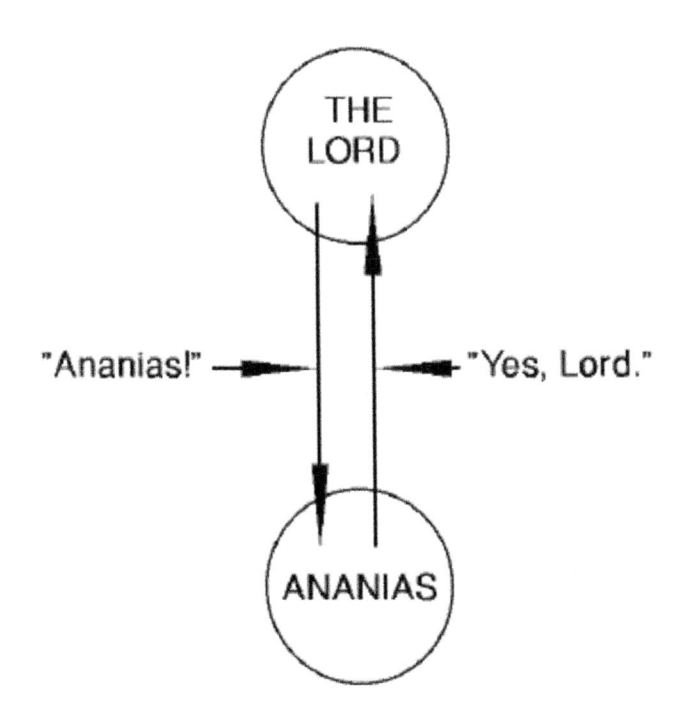

```
                    ┌──────┐
                    │ THE  │
                    │ LORD │
                    └──────┘
                       ↕
                    ┌──────┐
                    │ANANIAS│
                    └──────┘
```

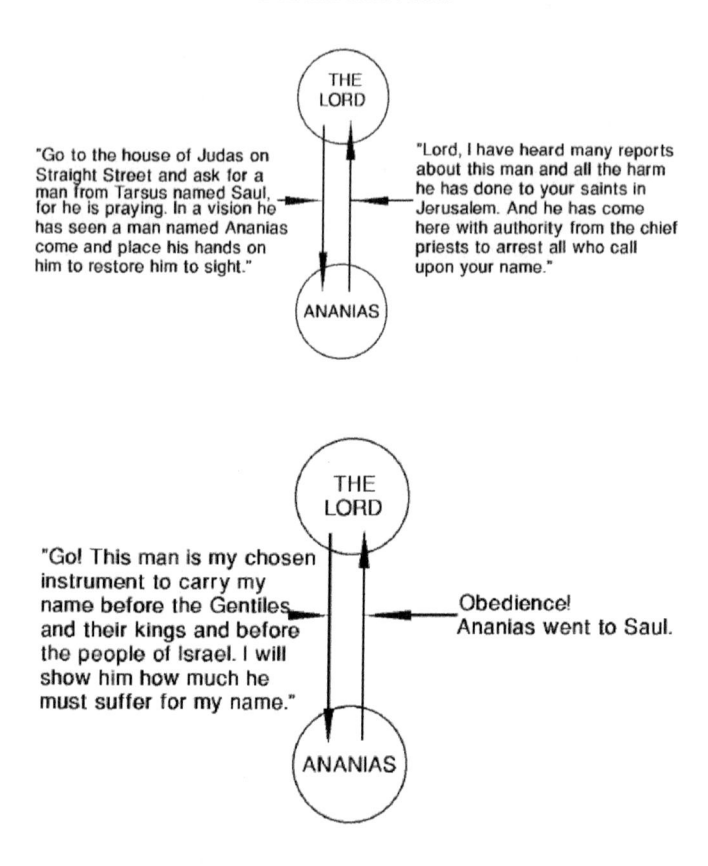

"Go to the house of Judas on Straight Street and ask for a man from Tarsus named Saul, for he is praying. In a vision he has seen a man named Ananias come and place his hands on him to restore him to sight."

"Lord, I have heard many reports about this man and all the harm he has done to your saints in Jerusalem. And he has come here with authority from the chief priests to arrest all who call upon your name."

```
                    ┌──────┐
                    │ THE  │
                    │ LORD │
                    └──────┘
                       ↕
                    ┌──────┐
                    │ANANIAS│
                    └──────┘
```

"Go! This man is my chosen instrument to carry my name before the Gentiles and their kings and before the people of Israel. I will show him how much he must suffer for my name."

Obedience! Ananias went to Saul.

SAUL STARTED HIS CHRISTIAN LIFE IN THE SCHOOL OF WAITING

The day on which Saul believed, that same day he enrolled in the school of Waiting On God In Prayer. His first lesson in the School lasted three days. He was praying and waiting on God for three days! For those three days he did nothing else but pray and wait on the Lord!

It was an auspicious start!

Is it surprising that he went so far with God?

For waiting on God in prayer, he received the following within three days of his conversion:

1. A vision.
2. Healing.
3. Revelation of what he was to do with his life.
4. Baptism into water.
5. Baptism into the Holy Spirit.

What if he had not waited on God in prayer? He would have missed all the above. He would have started his Christian life on a lower plane, and the entire course of his life and ministry might never have been what it became.

For those who are serious with God, waiting on Him in prayer is imperative!

Are you serious with God?

What are you doing about waiting on Him in prayer?

WAITING ON THE LORD IN PRAYER: THE EXAMPLE OF SAUL OF TARSUS - 2

"Now get up and stand on your feet. I have appeared to you to appoint you as a servant and as a witness of what you have seen of me and what I will show you" (Acts 26:16).

"I want you to know, brothers, that the gospel I preach is not something that man made up. I did not receive it from any man, nor was I taught it; rather, I received it by revelation from Jesus Christ" (Galatians 1:12).

"But when God, who set me apart from birth and called me by his grace, was pleased to reveal his Son in me so that I might preach him among the Gentiles, I did not consult any man, nor did I go up to Jerusalem to see those who were apostles before I was, but I went immediately into Arabia and later returned to Damascus. Then after three years, I went up to Jerusalem to get acquainted with Peter and

WAITING ON THE LORD IN PRAYER

stayed with him fifteen days" (Galatians 1:15-18).

From the very beginning, Saul of Tarsus knew that what he had seen of the Lord Jesus was just a part of the whole. He was told that more would be shown to him.

He knew, therefore, that if more was to be shown to him, he had to wait on God in prayer for things to be shown to him.

He waited on God in prayer to receive the Gospel he preached. Soon after his conversion he went into Arabia to wait on God in prayer. We do not know how long he was in Arabia, but he must have gone there to wait on God, so as to receive revelation. He might have wanted to ask the Lord the things that he did not understand, so as to receive answers from the Lord. As he waited before the Lord in prayer, he asked the Lord questions and received God's answers.

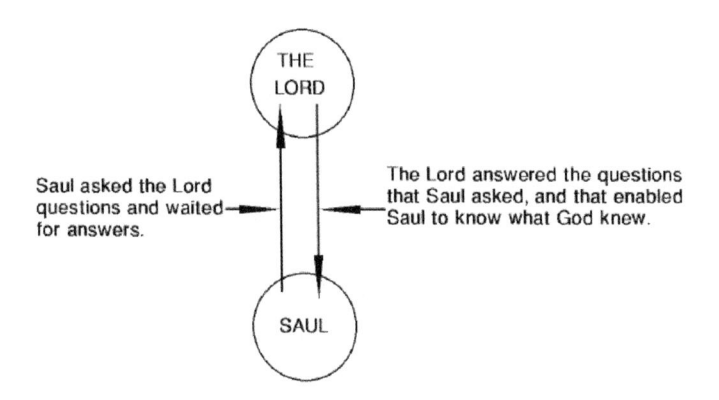

```
          THE
          LORD
           ○
           ↑↓
Saul asked the Lord           The Lord answered the questions
questions and waited →     ←  that Saul asked, and that enabled
for answers.                  Saul to know what God knew.
           ↕
          SAUL
           ○
```

Saul's commitment to the Lord Jesus was radical from the beginning and grew very rapidly. There is no doubt that as the Lord Jesus revealed Himself to him, he hungered more for Him. As he hungered more for Him, he sought him more and waited more on Him in prayer, which resulted in further revelation and then in further waiting in prayer.

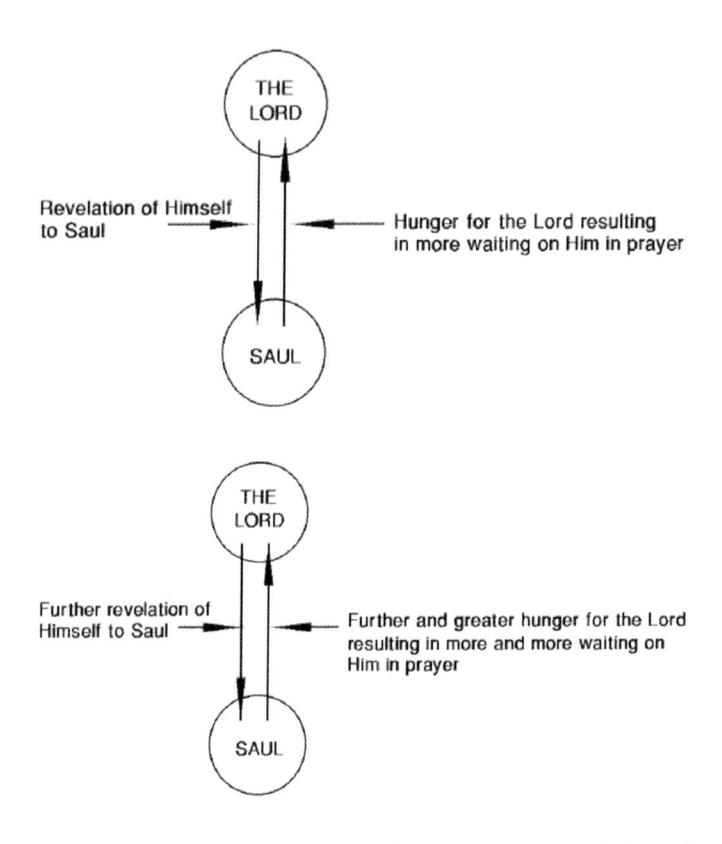

```
                    THE
                    LORD

Revelation of Himself          Hunger for the Lord resulting
to Saul                         in more waiting on Him in prayer

                    SAUL


                    THE
                    LORD

Further revelation of          Further and greater hunger for the Lord
Himself to Saul                resulting in more and more waiting on
                               Him in prayer

                    SAUL
```

What occupied Saul of Tarsus in the three years that followed his return to Damascus after his stay in Arabia? We say emphatically that they were three years given to waiting on God in prayer. He must have prayed, then waited on God, heard God and prayed some more. And this went on and on for three years before he went to Jerusalem to get acquainted with the Apostle Peter!

Gordon Lindsay has this to say about this matter:

"Every man, after he has been converted to Christ ,would do well to set aside a period of time in which he waits before God, studies His Word, and seeks the Divine will for his life. What a boon it would be to every believer if during the formative period of his Christian life, he devoted a special time to be alone with God! How many heartaches and blunders would be avoided!

Education is a valuable tool, and Paul had the best available of his day. Knowledge on how to make a living is important, and Paul had that. But what he learned out in the Arabian desert had a value far surpassing these things. Galatians 1:15-18, informs us of the so-called "silent period" in Paul's life. After he had given his powerful and striking testimony in the city of Damascus, the young man departed from the haunts of society and isolated himself in the Arabian desert. Not until three years had passed, did he return. By then he had more than a testimony. He had a full revelation of the gospel which he unfolded in detail in his epistles. There as he waited before God, the Lord revealed to him the body of truth that he was to deliver to the church."

— GORDON LINDSAY, "PRAYING TO CHANGE THE WORLD," VOLUME 2, DALLAS, TEXAS, U.S.A

16

A PRAYER MEETING WITH WAITING ON THE LORD IN PRAYER

In a normal prayer meeting, believers come with various burdens, and when they are permitted, they begin to pour these burdens on the Lord. There is nothing wrong with this, since the Lord has asked us to ask and we will receive.

However, these types of prayer meetings are dominated by the thoughts of man and the needs of man. They carry the burden of man.

Meanwhile, besides the burdens of man, there are the burdens of the Lord!

The Bible, in speaking of the burden of the Lord, said,

> "And when this people, or the prophet, or priest, shall ask thee, saying, What is the burden of the Lord? Thou shalt then say unto them, What burden? I will even forsake you, saith the Lord. And as for the prophet, and the priest, and the people, that shall say, The burden of the Lord, I will even punish that man and his house…… And the burden

of the Lord shall ye mention no more; for every man's word shall be his burden, for ye have perverted the words of the living God, of the Lord of hosts our God...... But since ye say, The burden of the Lord; therefore thus saith the Lord; Because ye say this word, The burden of the Lord, and I have sent unto you, saying, Ye shall not say, The burden of the Lord" (Jeremiah 23:33-36).

If believers came to the Prayer Meeting and waited on the Lord in prayer, He would deliver them from their own burdens and then put His own burdens on them, and they would pray His burdens through.

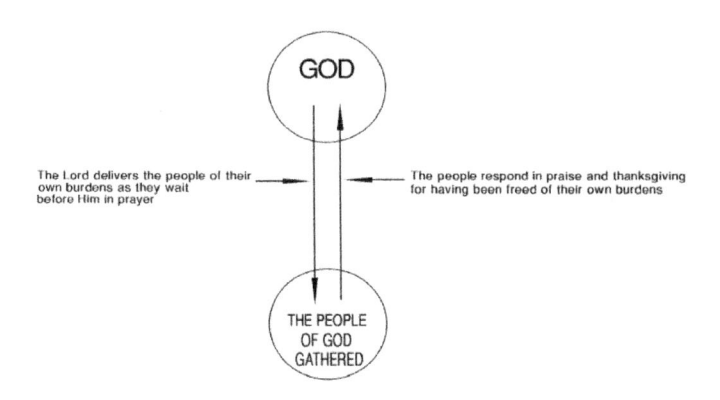

```
                    GOD

The Lord delivers the people of their        The people respond in praise and thanksgiving
own burdens as they wait                     for having been freed of their own burdens
before Him in prayer

                THE PEOPLE
                  OF GOD
                 GATHERED
```

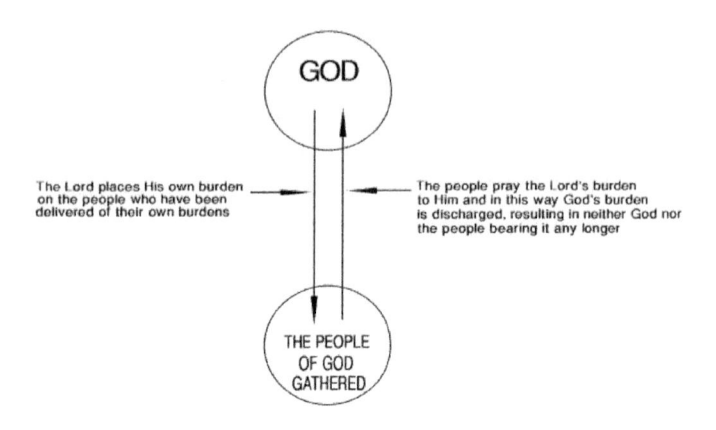

```
                    ┌─────┐
                    │ GOD │
                    └─────┘
                       ↑↓
The Lord places His own burden          The people pray the Lord's burden
on the people who have been             to Him and in this way God's burden
delivered of their own burdens          is discharged, resulting in neither God nor
                                        the people bearing it any longer

                 ┌──────────┐
                 │THE PEOPLE│
                 │  OF GOD  │
                 │ GATHERED │
                 └──────────┘
```

If the people of God came to pray for six hours, and they all waited on the Lord in prayer, everyone could be tuned to the Holy Spirit and thus plugged into the spirit of the meeting. The waiting on God to deliver them could begin. Some would be delivered immediately and receive the Lord's burden and start to labour in prayer that His burden be discharged. Others would wait on the Lord longer before they could know deliverance from their own burdens and before they could receive the Lord's burden.

It could be that after three hours, everyone would have been delivered of his own burden and put on God's burden. It would mean that the last three hours would be spent labouring to discharge the burden of the Lord. This is wonderful.

There are times when the Holy Spirit will place just one of the Lord's burdens on everyone gathered. Consequently, everyone would be carrying the same burden and praying for the same thing. This is wonderful.

It could be that the entire six hours are spent waiting before the Lord for the discharge of personal burdens. This would mean that all is silence and there is no asking that day. It could be that the next Prayer Meeting of six hours is all spent receiving the Lord's burden. This would mean that there would be no asking at that meeting. People would receive God's burden and then go away to meditate more on it. The third Prayer Meeting would be for asking that the Lord's burden be lifted and everyone would pray with all his heart until the burden of the Lord is lifted.

This would all be wonderful.

It could be that instead of the Lord laying His burden on the saints, He lays on them one of their own burdens. The procedure would be the same.

May the Lord lead the church more and more into this type of praying! It will surely be answered! Amen.

WAITING ON THE LORD IN PRAYER: THE EXAMPLE OF THE LORD JESUS

"Jesus, full of the Holy Spirit, returned from the
 Jordan and was led by the Spirit in the desert,
 where for forty days he was tempted by the devil.
 He ate nothing during those days, and at the end
 of them he was hungry......
Jesus returned to Galilee in the power of the Spirit,
 and news about him spread through the whole
 countryside. He taught in their synagogue and
 everyone praised him»(Luke 4:1-15).

The Lord Jesus knew that the three and a half years of ministry that were before Him were critically important. He had been preparing for it for the last thirty years. Recently, He had undergone further preparation by being baptized in water, having the Holy Spirit come upon Him and having the approval of His Father!

He needed some more time of waiting before His Father in prayer! He was led by the Holy Spirit to wait on the Lord God Almighty in prayer and fasting.

Deep things must have been received from His Father as He waited in fasting. Great blows and knock-outs were also lashed out to the devil as He waited and fasted.

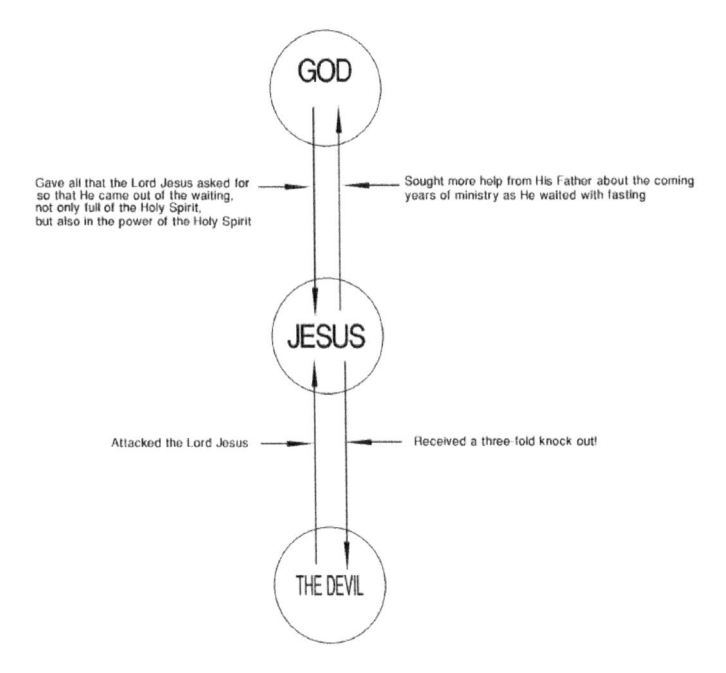

```
                        GOD
                         ↑↓

Gave all that the Lord Jesus asked for          Sought more help from His Father about the coming
so that He came out of the waiting,             years of ministry as He waited with fasting
not only full of the Holy Spirit,
but also in the power of the Holy Spirit

                        JESUS
                         ↑↓

Attacked the Lord Jesus                         Received a three-fold knock out!

                      THE DEVIL
```

There is fasting which is total abstention from food. That has value. There is also fasting that is both total abstention from food and withdrawal from human company. That has added value. There is fasting that is total abstention from food, total abstention from human company and total investment on waiting on God in prayer. This is the best and this is what the Lord Jesus carried out. Is there any wonder that it had such far-reaching consequences?

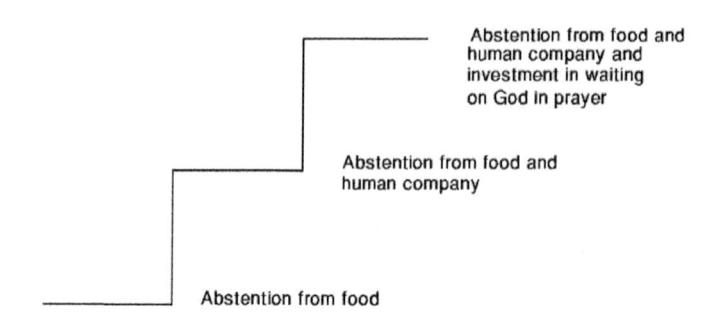

Abstention from food and human company and investment in waiting on God in prayer

Abstention from food and human company

Abstention from food

We encourage fasting saints to consider adding the dimensions of withdrawal from human company and total investment in waiting on God in prayer.

We know that the waiting on God is a richer experience when accompanied by fasting, because fasting "subdues" the flesh and gives freedom to the spirit.

Go and do what the Lord did.

Amen.

18
IN CONCLUSION

We recommend that even if you have only five minutes to spend in prayer, you should invest three minutes in waiting on the Lord and two minutes on talking to Him. This will cause the five minutes to count more than if all the five were spent on carrying out a monologue with yourself.

VERY IMPORTANT!!!

If you have not yet received Jesus as your Lord and Saviour, I encourage you to receive Him. Here are some steps to help you,

ADMIT that you are a sinner by nature and by practice and that on your own you are without hope. Tell God you have personally sinned against Him in your thoughts, words and deeds. Confess your sins to Him, one after another in a sincere prayer. Do not leave out any sins that you can remember. Truly turn from your sinful ways and abandon them. If you stole, steal no more. If you have been committing adultery or fornication, stop it. God will not forgive you if you have no desire to stop sinning in all areas of your life, but if you are sincere, He will give you the power to stop sinning.

BELIEVE that Jesus Christ, who is God's Son, is the only Way, the only Truth and the only Life. Jesus said,

> *"I am the way, the truth and the life; no one comes to the Father, but by me"* (John 14:6).

VERY IMPORTANT!!!

The Bible says,

> *"For there is one God, and there is one mediator between God and men, the man Christ Jesus, who gave himself as a ransom for all" (1 Timothy 2:5-6).*

> *"And there is salvation in no one else (apart from Jesus), for there is no other name under heaven given among men by which we must be saved" (Acts 4:12).*

> *But to all who received him, who believed in his name, he gave power to become children of God..." (John 1:12).*

BUT,

CONSIDER the cost of following Him. Jesus said that all who follow Him must deny themselves, and this includes selfish financial, social and other interests. He also wants His followers to take up their crosses and follow Him. Are you prepared to abandon your own interests daily for those of Christ? Are you prepared to be led in a new direction by Him? Are you prepared to suffer for Him and die for Him if need be? Jesus will have nothing to do with half-hearted people. His demands are total. He will only receive and forgive those who are prepared to follow Him AT ANY COST. Think about it and count the cost. If you are prepared to follow Him, come what may, then there is something to do.

INVITE Jesus to come into your heart and life. He says,

> *"Behold I stand at the door and knock. If anyone hears my voice and opens the door (to his heart and life), I will come in to him and eat with him, and he with me "* (Revelation 3:20).

VERY IMPORTANT!!!

Why don't you pray a prayer like the following one or one of your own construction as the Holy Spirit leads?

> *"Lord Jesus, I am a wretched, lost sinner who has sinned in thought, word and deed. Forgive all my sins and cleanse me. Receive me, Saviour and transform me into a child of God. Come into my heart now and give me eternal life right now. I will follow you at all costs, trusting the Holy Spirit to give me all the power I need."*

When you pray this prayer sincerely, Jesus answers at once and justifies you before God and makes you His child.

> *Please write to us (**ztfbooks@cmfionline.org**) and I will pray for you and help you as you go on with Jesus Christ.*

THANK YOU

For Reading This Book

If you have any question and/or need help, do not hesitate to contact us through **ztfbooks@cmfionline.org**. If the book has blessed you, then we would also be grateful if you leave a positive review at your favorite retailer.

ZTF BOOKS, through Christian Publishing House (CPH) offers a wide selection of best selling Christian books (in print, eBook & audiobook formats) on a broad spectrum of topics, including marriage & family, sexuality, practical spiritual warfare, Christian service, Christian leadership, and much more. Visit us at **ztfbooks.com** to learn more about our latest releases and special offers. **And thank you for being a ZTF BOOK reader**.

We invite you to connect with more from the author through social media (**cmfionline**) and/or ministry website (**ztfministry.org**), where we offer both on-ground and remote training courses (all year round) from basic to university level at the **University of Prayer and Fasting (WUPF)** and the **School of Knowing and Serving God (SKSG)**. You are highly welcome to enrol at your soonest convenience. A **FREE online Bible Course** is also available.

Finally, we would like to recommend to you another suitable title - The Ministry Of Supplication:

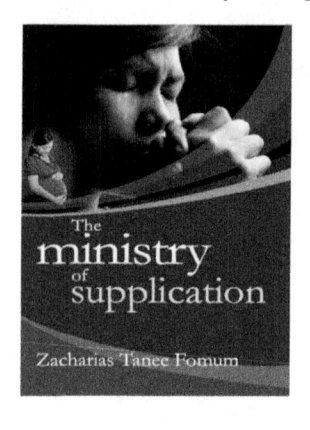

God answers prayers. If people are desperate enough to seek His will, know what He wants and then wrestle to see it come to reality, it will become a reality. Hannah had a problem. Her problem was a kind of national problem because the nation desperately needed a prophet, and her first son had to occupy that post and function in that office. Initially, she was complacent in her barrenness, but the ministry of provocation, which she received from Peninnah, stirred her to wrestle with tears, fasting, vowing, more tears, bitterness of soul, anguish of soul, great anguish and great grief, until she moved God to hear her and answer her.

In moving God to provide her need, she also moved God to provide the need of His people.

May the Lord mightily touch you as you read this book! May it move you to abandon all that must be abandoned in order that you may be abundantly fruitful! May your eyes be opened to your potential to execute God's will by seeing His cause, making His cause your cause and asking Him to move through your supplication to make an individual, a family, a town, a nation, nations and continents of the earth your possession for Him!

ABOUT THE AUTHOR

Professor Zacharias Tanee Fomum was born in the flesh on 20th June 1945 and became born again on 13th June 1956. On 1st October 1966, He consecrated his life to the Lord Jesus and to His service, and was filled with the Holy Spirit on 24th October 1970. He was taken to be with the Lord on 14th March, 2009.

Pr Fomum was admitted to a first class in the Bachelor of Science degree, graduating as a prize winning student from Fourah Bay College in the University of Sierra Leone in October 1969. At the age of 28, he was awarded a Ph.D. in Organic Chemistry by the University of Makerere, Kampala in Uganda. In October 2005, he was awarded a Doctor of Science (D.Sc) by the University of Durham, Great Britain. This higher doctorate was in recognition of his distinct contributions to scientific knowledge through research. As a Professor of Organic Chemistry in the University of Yaoundé 1, Cameroon, Professor Fomum supervised or co-supervised more than 100 Master's Degree and Doctoral Degree theses and co-authored over 160 scientific articles in leading international journals. He considered Jesus Christ the Lord of Science ("For by Him all things were created..." – Colossians 1:16), and scientific research an act of obedience to God's command to "subdue the earth" (Genesis 1:28). He therefore made the Lord Jesus the Director of his research laboratory while he took the place of deputy director, and attributed his outstanding success as a scientist to Jesus' revelational leadership.

In more than 40 years of Christian ministry, Pr Fomum travelled extensively, preaching the Gospel, planting churches and training spiritual leaders. He made more than:

- 700 missionary journeys within Cameroon, which ranged from one day to three weeks in duration.
- 500 missionary journeys to more than 70 different nations in all the six continents. These ranged from two days to six weeks in duration.

By the time of his going to be with the Lord in 2009, he had preached in over 1000 localities in Cameroon, sent over 200 national missionaries into many localities in Cameroon and planted over 1300 churches in the various administrative provinces of Cameroon. At his base in Yaoundé, he planted and built a mega-church with his co-workers which grew to a steady membership of about 12,000. Pr Fomum was the founding team-leader of Christian Missionary Fellowship International (CMFI); an evangelism, soul-winning, disciple making, Church-planting and missionary-sending movement with more than 200 international missionaries and thousands of churches in 65 nations spread across Africa, Europe, the Americas, Asia and Oceania. In the course of their ministry, Pr Fomum and his team witnessed more than 10,000 recorded healing miracles performed by God in answer to prayer in the name of Jesus Christ. These miracles include instant healings of headaches, cancers, HIV/AIDS, blindness, deafness, dumbness, paralysis, madness, and new teeth and organs received.

Pr Fomum read the entire Bible more than 60 times, read more than 1350 books on the Christian faith and authored over 150 books to advance the Gospel of Jesus Christ. 5 million copies of these books are in circulation in 12 languages as well as 16 million gospel tracts in 17 languages.

Pr Fomum was a man who sought God. He spent between 15 minutes and six hours daily alone with God in what he called Daily Dynamic Encounters with God (DDEWG). During these DDEWG he read God's Word, meditated on it, listened to God's voice, heard God speak to him, recorded what God was saying to him and prayed it through. He thus had over 18,000 DDEWG. He also had over 60 periods of withdrawing to seek God alone for periods that ranged from 3 to 21 days (which he termed Retreats for Spiritual Progress). The time he spent seeking God slowly transformed him into a man who hungered, thirsted and panted after God. His unceasing heart cry was: "Oh, that I would have more of God!"

Pr Fomum was a man of prayer and a leading teacher on prayer in many churches and conferences around the world. He considered prayer to be the most important work that can be done for God and for man. He was a man of faith who believed that God answers prayer. He kept a record of his prayer requests and had over 50, 000 recorded answers to prayer in his prayer books. He carried out over 100 Prayer Walks of between five and forty-seven kilometres in towns and cities around the world. He and his team carried out over 57 Prayer Crusades (periods of forty days and nights during which at least eight hours are invested into prayer each day). They also carried out over 80 Prayer Sieges (times of near non-stop praying that ranges from 24 hours to 120 hours). He authored the Prayer Power Series, a 13-volume set of books on various aspects of prayer; Supplication, Fasting, Intercession and Spiritual Warfare. He started prayer chains, prayer rooms, prayer houses, national and continental prayer movements in Cameroon and other nations. He worked with leaders of local churches in India to disciple and train more than 2 million believers.

Pr Fomum also considered fasting as one of the weapons of Christian Spiritual Warfare. He carried out over 250 fasts ranging from three days to forty days, drinking only water or water supplemented with soluble vitamins. Called by the Lord to a distinct ministry of intercession, he pioneered fasting and prayer movements and led in battles against principalities and powers obstructing the progress of the Gospel and God's global purposes. He was enabled to carry out 3 supra – long fasts of between 52 and 70 days in his final years.

Pr Fomum chose a lifestyle of simplicity and "self- imposed poverty" in order to invest more funds into the critical work of evangelism, soul winning, church-planting and the building up of believers. Knowing the importance of money and its role in the battle to reach those without Christ with the glorious Gospel, he and his wife grew to investing 92.5% of their earned income from all sources (salaries, allowances, royalties and cash gifts) into the Gospel. They invested with the hope that, as they grew in the knowledge and the love of the Lord, and the perishing souls of people, they would one day invest 99% of their income into the Gospel.

He was married to Prisca Zei Fomum and they had seven children who are all involved in the work of the Gospel, some serving as missionaries. Prisca is a national and international minister, specializing in the winning and discipling of children to Jesus Christ. She also communicates and imparts the vision of ministry to children with a view to raising and building up ministers to them.

The Professor owed all that he was and all that God had done through him, to the unmerited favour and blessing of God and to his worldwide army of friends and co-workers. He considered himself nothing without them and the blessing of God; and would have amounted to nothing but for them. All praise and glory to Jesus Christ!

- facebook.com/cmfionline
- twitter.com/cmfionline
- instagram.com/cmfionline
- pinterest.com/cmfionline
- youtube.com/cmfionline

ALSO BY Z.T. FOMUM

Online Catalog: https://ztfbooks.com

THE CHRISTIAN WAY

1. The Way Of Life
2. The Way Of Obedience
3. The Way Of Discipleship
4. The Way Of Sanctification
5. The Way Of Christian Character
6. The Way Of Spiritual Power
7. The Way Of Christian Service
8. The Way Of Spiritual Warfare
9. The Way Of Suffering For Christ
10. The Way Of Victorious Praying
11. The Way Of Overcomers
12. The Way Of Spiritual Encouragement
13. The Way Of Loving The Lord

THE PRAYER POWER SERIES

1. The Way Of Victorious Praying
2. The Ministry Of Fasting
3. The Art Of Intercession
4. The Practice Of Intercession
5. Praying With Power
6. Practical Spiritual Warfare Through Prayer
7. Moving God Through Prayer
8. The Ministry Of Praise And Thanksgiving
9. Waiting On The Lord In Prayer

10. The Ministry Of Supplication
11. Life-Changing Thoughts On Prayer, Volume 1
12. The Centrality Of Prayer
13. Spiritual Aggressiveness
14. Life-Changing Thoughts On Prayer, Volume 2
15. Prayer and Spiritual Intimacy
16. Life-Changing Thoughts on Prayer Volume 3
17. The Art of Worship

PRACTICAL HELPS FOR OVERCOMERS

1. Discipleship at any cost
2. The Use Of Time
3. Retreats For Spiritual Progress
4. Personal Spiritual Revival
5. Daily Dynamic Encounters With God
6. The School Of Truth
7. How To Succeed In The Christian Life
8. The Christian And Money
9. Deliverance From The Sin Of Laziness
10. The Art Of Working Hard
11. Knowing God - The Greatest Need Of The Hour
12. Revelation: A Must
13. True Repentance
14. Restitution - An Important Message For The Overcomers
15. You Can Receive A Pure Heart Today
16. You Can Lead Someone To The Lord Jesus Today
17. You Can Receive The Baptism Into The Holy Spirit Now
18. The Dignity Of Manual Labour
19. You Have A Talent!
20. The Making Of Disciples

21. The Secret Of Spiritual Fruitfulness
22. Are You Still A Disciple Of The Lord Jesus?
23. The Overcomer As A Servant Of Man

GOD, SEX AND YOU

1. Enjoying The Premarital Life
2. **Enjoying The Choice Of Your Marriage Partner**
3. Enjoying The Married Life
4. **Divorce And Remarriage**
5. A Successful Marriage; The Husband's Making
6. A Successful Marriage; The Wife's Making

RECENT TITLES BY THE ZTF EDITORIAL TEAM

1. Power For Service
2. The Art Of Worship
3. Issues Of The Heart
4. In The Crucible For Service
5. Spiritual Nobility
6. Roots And Destinies
7. Revolutionary Thoughts On Spiritual Leadership
8. The Leader And His God
9. The Overthrow Of Principalities And Powers
10. Walking With God (Vol. 1)
11. God Centeredness
12. Victorious Dispositions
13. The Believer's Conscience
14. The Processes Of Faith
15. Spiritual Gifts
16. The Missionary As A Son

17. You, Your Team And Your Ministry
18. Prayer And A Walk With God
19. Leading A Local Church
20. Church Planting Strategies
21. The Character And The Personality of The Leader
22. Deliverance From The Sin of Gluttony
23. The Spirit Filled Life
24. The Church: Rights And Responsibilities Of The Believer
25. Thoughts On Marriage
26. Learning To Importune In Prayer
27. Jesus Saves And Heals Today
28. God, Money And You
29. Meet The Liberator
30. Salvation And Soul Winning
31. The Salvation Of The Lord Jesus: Soul Winning (Vol. 3)
32. Soul Winning And The Making Of Disciples
33. Victorious Soul Winning
34. Making Spiritual Progress (Vol. 4)
35. Life Changing Thought On Prayer (Vol. 3)
36. Knowing God And Walking With Him
37. What Our Ministry Is
38. Practical Dying To Self And The Spirit-filled Life
39. Leading God's People
40. Laws Of Spiritual Leadership
41. From His Lips: Compilation of Autobiographical Notes on Professor Zacharias Tanee Fomum
42. The School of Soul Winners and Soul Winning
43. The Complete Work of Zacharias Tanee Fomum on Prayer (Volume 1)
44. Knowing and Serving God (Volume 2)
45. Walking With God (Volume 1)

PRACTICAL HELPS IN SANCTIFICATION

1. Deliverance From Sin
2. The Way Of Sanctification
3. Sanctified And Consecrated For Spiritual Ministry
4. The Sower, The Seed And The Hearts Of Men
5. Freedom From The Sin Of Adultery And Fornication
6. The Sin Before You May Lead To Immediate Death: Do Not Commit It!
7. Be Filled With The Holy Spirit
8. The Power Of The Holy Spirit In The Winning Of The Lost

MAKING SPIRITUAL PROGRESS

1. Vision, Burden, Action
2. The Ministers And The Ministry of The New Covenant
3. The Cross In The Life And Ministry Of The Believer
4. Knowing The God Of Unparalleled Goodness
5. Brokenness: The Secret Of Spiritual Overflow
6. The Secret Of Spiritual Rest
7. Making Spiritual Progress, Volume 1
8. Making Spiritual Progress, Volume 2
9. Making Spiritual Progress, Volume 3
10. Making Spiritual Progress, Volume 4

EVANGELISM

1. God's Love And Forgiveness

2. The Way Of Life
3. Come Back Home My Son; I Still Love You
4. Jesus Loves You And Wants To Heal You
5. Come And See; Jesus Has Not Changed!
6. 36 Reasons For Winning The Lost To Christ
7. Soul Winning, Volume 1
8. Soul Winning, Volume 2
9. Celebrity A Mask

UNCATEGORISE

1. Laws Of Spiritual Success, Volume 1
2. The Shepherd And The Flock
3. Deliverance From Demons
4. Inner Healing
5. No Failure Needs To Be Final
6. Facing Life's Problems Victoriously
7. A Word To The Students
8. The Prophecy Of The Overthrow Of The Satanic Prince Of Cameroon
9. Basic Christian Leadership
10. A Missionary life and a missionary heart
11. Power to perform miracles

WOMEN OF THE GLORY

1. **The Secluded Worshipper**: The Life, Ministry, And Glorification Of The Prophetess Anna
2. **Unending Intimacy**: The Transformation, Choices And Overflow of Mary of Bethany
3. **Winning Love:** The rescue, development and fulfilment of Mary Magdalene

4. **Not Meant for Defeat**: The Rise, Battles, and Triumph of Queen Esther

ZTF COMPLETE WORKS

1. The School of Soul Winners and Soul Winning
2. The Complete Works of Zacharias Tanee Fomum on Prayer (Volume 1)
3. The Complete Works of Zacharias Tanee Fomum on Leadership (Volume 1)
4. The Complete Works of Z.T Fomum on Marriage
5. Making Spiritual Progress (The Complete Box Set of Four Volumes)

OTHER TITLES

1. A Broken Vessel
2. The Joy of Begging to Belong to the Lord Jesus Christ: A Testimony

ZTF AUTO-BIOGRAPHIES

1. From His Lips: About The Author
2. From His Lips: About His Co-Workers
3. From His Lips: Back From His Missions
4. From His Lips: About Our Ministry
5. From His Lips: On Our Vision
6. From His Lips: School of Knowing & Serving God

DISTRIBUTORS OF ZTF BOOKS

These books can be obtained in French and English Language from any of the following distribution outlets:

EDITIONS DU LIVRE CHRETIEN (ELC)

- **Location:** Paris, France
- **Email:** editionlivrechretien@gmail.com
- **Phone:** +33 6 98 00 90 47

INTERNET

- **Location:** on all major online **eBook, Audiobook** and **print-on-demand** (paperback) retailers (Amazon, Google, iBooks, B&N, Ingram, NotionPress, etc.).
- **Email**: ztfbooks@cmfionline.org
- **Phone**: +47 454 12 804
- **Website**: ztfbooks.com

CPH YAOUNDE

- **Location:** Yaounde, Cameroon
- **Email:** editionsztf@gmail.com
- **Phone:** +237 74756559

ZTF LITERATURE AND MEDIA HOUSE

- **Location:** Lagos, Nigeria
- **Email:** zlmh@ztfministry.org
- **Phone:** +2348152163063

CPH BURUNDI

- **Location:** Bujumbura, Burundi
- **Email:** cph-burundi@ztfministry.org
- **Phone:** +257 79 97 72 75

CPH UGANDA

- **Location:** Kampala, Uganda
- **Email:** cph-uganda@ztfministry.org
- **Phone:** +256 785 619613

CPH SOUTH AFRICA

- **Location:** Johannesburg, RSA
- **Email:** tantohtantoh@yahoo.com
- **Phone**: +27 83 744 5682

Printed in Great Britain
by Amazon